CONTENTS

Page

ILLUSTRATIONS iii

PREFACE iv

ABSTRACT vi

WHO ARE THE CUBANS? 1
    The First Cubans: Native Americans 1
    The Cuban Ancestry: The Spanish 3
        The Spanish Empire 4
        The Explorers 5
        The Conquerors (Conquistadores) 6
        The Colonists 7
        The African Slaves 8
    Three Cultures, One People 12

CASTRO'S RISE TO POWER 16

CASTRO'S SUCCESS 45

CASTRO'S CONTINUED SURVIVAL 58
    SOCIO-ECONOMIC FACTORS 58
        The Economic System 58
        The Medical System 66
        The Education System 69
        Land Distribution Policy 70
        Social Structure 74
    US POLICY 77
        Background 77

PAST CUBA POLICY 89
    EISENHOWER ADMINISTRATION 89
    THE KENNEDY ADMINISTRATION 90
    THE JOHNSON ADMINISTRATION 96
    THE NIXON ADMINISTRATION 97
    THE FORD ADMINISTRATION 99

THE CARTER ADMINISTRATION 100
THE REAGAN ADMINISTRATION 102
THE BUSH ADMINISTRATION 105

CURRENT CUBA POLICY AND SCENARIOS FOR CHANGE IN CUBA...............113
THE CLINTON ADMINISTRATION 113
SCENARIOS FOR POLITICAL CHANGE IN CUBA............................117

ASSESSMENT OF THE CURRENT POLICY 132

PROPOSAL FOR POLICY REVIEW PROCESS 146

CONCLUSION...155

BIBLIOGRAPHY...157

ILLUSTRATIONS

Page

Figure 1. Cuba Matrix……………………………………………………………..152
Figure 2. Cuba Matrix Sub-Committees…………………………………………..153
Figure 3. Cuba Matrix Executive Board…………………………………………..154

Preface

Why did Cuba, the "Pearl of the Antilles," succumb to the allure of a false messiah? Why has "Castroism"[1] survived in the shadow of the world's most powerful capitalist nation? What lies ahead for the eleven million people who have for the past forty-one years been deprived of their right to "life, liberty, and the pursuit of happiness?"

These and many other questions has been the subject of countless books written by scholars, politicians and academicians of the Eastern, Western, Northern and Southern hemispheres. The approaches have differed and, as one might expect, each is affected by the author's unique perspective. This paper is different if only because it is written by a woman who was born in Cuba in 1959 and who has felt honored to "support and defend the Constitution of the United States" as a commissioned officer in the United States Air Force.

As the daughter of first generation Cubans, I was fortunate to have been a silent participant in discussions on political and economic relations between the "Mother Country," Spain, and Cuba. Later, I would hear much about the betrayal of "one of our own," Fidel Castro, and of hopes shattered by President John F. Kennedy. These things did not mean much to me as a little girl. I knew that we were often hungry, that Santa Claus did not visit Cuba and that if I closed my eyes and prayed to God for a piece of

---

[1]Andres Suarez, *Cuba: Castroism and Communism, 1959-1966* (Cambridge, Massachusetts: The Massachusetts Institute of Technology Press, 1967), 78.

candy I did not get it. However, when I closed my eyes and prayed to Fidel Castro the piece of candy appeared in the hand of none other than my third grade teacher.

Thirty-three years later, I embarked on this journey to find the answers to the questions I presented. It is my hope that my journey will serve to enlighten those who, like me, are not familiar with the political, social, and economic history of that tiny little island ninety miles South of the Florida coast that has on so many occasions been at the center of international events. I must acknowledge that the time constraints on this project did not allow me to do it justice. I encourage those whose interest I may spark, to conduct further reading from the list of references provided.

I would like to thank Dr. Jaime Suchlicki and Dr. Andy Gomez of the School of International Studies at the University of Miami for their invaluable guidance and assistance with this project. I would also like to extend my gratitude to my family for their support over the past year and to my son, Jason, for his invaluable assistance with the computer software.

Abstract

The first part of this paper uses a historic perspective as a starting point for discussion of the factors that, in the author's opinion, contributed to Fidel Castro's rise to power in 1959. The focus of the historic analysis will be on those events that shaped Cuban culture and affected Cuba's political development from 1492 to 1898. The second part of the paper covers the political and socio-economic events leading to Castro's ascension to power. Part Three reviews the theories purported to have contributed to the success of "Castroism" and Part Four analyzes the factors that have contributed to its continued survival. In Part Five, the analysis focuses on past US policy and its effect on the Castro regime. The current Cuba policy and proposed scenarios for political change are covered in Part Six turning to an assessment of the current policy in Part 7. The paper concludes with a proposal for a new policy review process in Part 8.

PART I

WHO ARE THE CUBANS?

In order to determine why Cuba finds itself in its present state and to begin to imagine what its future might be, it is critical to understand the cultural and historical background of its people. Therefore, this paper starts at the beginning.

The First Cubans: Native Americans

It is generally accepted that Cuba's first inhabitants were the Ciboney (or Guanahacabibe) Indians who arrived by sea following the trade winds westward from the coast of Venezuela along the islands of the Caribbean.[1] The Ciboney began to settle the island about 1000 B.C. and lived along the coast in caves.[2] They survived by fishing, hunting, and gathering plant foods. They were also highly competent stone workers. They lived in small, semi-nomadic clans and left no written record of their society, religion, or language. The little known about the Ciboney and those who followed, the Arawaks, comes from the writings of early explorers and archeological discoveries.[3]

The Arawaks reached Cuba in two waves beginning with the sub-Tainos in about 900 A.D.[4] They originated from the area around the Orinoco and Amazon rivers that are currently part of Venezuela and the Gaines.[5] The first wave of the Arawaks lived in thatched houses and survived by fishing and collectively working gardens where they grew fruit and vegetables. They also grew tobacco used in religious ceremonies.[6] The second wave of the Arawaks, the Tainos, arrived just before the Spanish conquest in the fifteenth century from the island of Hispaniola (the Dominican Republic and Haiti). They settled the Eastern coastal area of the island of Cuba.[7]

Unlike the Ciboney and sub-Taino cultures, the Taino culture that flourished developed advanced economic and social systems. They were skilled agrarians and expanded from the production of yucca to tobacco, cotton, corn, white and sweet potato. They also manufactured cotton textiles and pottery.[8] Taino society was a matrilineal society. Hereditary chiefs (caciques) ruled specific territories that were further subdivided and governed by lower-level chiefs. Below the chiefs was a mobility class in charge of community affairs. This class included the priests (behiques) or medicine men. The next class was that of the "commoner". This class represented the majority of Taino society with all associated rights and responsibilities. The lowest class, the Naborias, were life-long serfs who were unable to own property and received required sustenance in return for labor performed within the community.[9]

When Christopher Columbus reached the island in his first voyage to the Americas in 1492, Cuba's indigenous population numbered approximately 112,000 with about 92,000 sub-Tainos, 10,000 Tainos and 10,000 Ciboney.[10] The Indian culture was decimated by the Spanish and subsequently displaced by the emerging colonial, Criollo (Cuban-born Spaniards) and African cultures. In spite of the fact that the Ciboney and Arawaks inhabited Cuba for nearly a century and a half, with the exception of a few words and some foods, the indigenous native cultures failed to leave a lasting impression on the emerging colonial and Criollo cultures.[11]

The Cuban Ancestry: The Spanish

The Spanish Kingdom came to being in the fifteenth century when the European powers began to expand overseas in search of gold, raw materials, new markets and cheap labor. However, long before it grew into an empire, Spain was beset by many invaders who greatly impacted its cultural development. The most notable settlers were the Romans, the Arabs and the Jews. The Romans gave Spain the Latin language; however, it was Arabs, who arrived in 711 A.D. who made the most indelible contributions to the Spanish culture in the fields of science, agriculture and textiles. Likewise, the Jews also made significant intellectual contributions especially in the areas of literature and finance.[12] The Arab's governing structure, based on the all-powerful "caliph" (ruler), had a profound influence on the development of Spain's political system. The caliphs were absolute rulers on political and ecclesiastical matters. After centuries of Arab rule, the Spanish people came to depend on the "caliphs" to resolve all their problems. This dependence on a ruling authority absolved the people of responsibility for their own actions and placed the hope, credit, and blame upon the all-powerful ruler.[13]

Due to their intellectual and enterprising nature, by the early fifteenth century, Spain's socio-economic systems were largely in the hands of the Arabs and the Jews who actively pursued governmental, scientific and business ventures disdained by the Christian segment of Spanish society. In the name of religious and racial purity, the Jews were driven out of Spain in 1492 and the Arabs about a century later.[14] Although the Spanish considered the defeat of the Arabs the "Reconquest" [15] of their country, they chose to retain the Arab's political system making their king an all-powerful entity. The

3

Spanish shied away from work previously performed by the ousted castes. As a result, virtually all commerce and industry was destroyed. In lieu of the intellectual or business professions, the Spanish turned to the military, the priesthood, exploration and conquest in the newly discovered Americas.[16]

Religious intolerance was at the crux of the Inquisition chartered by Papal authority at the request of King Ferdinand V and Queen Isabella I in 1498. Originally, established to deal with the problem of Jews who had "insincerely converted to Christianity,"[17] the Inquisition would not be suppressed until 1834.[18] The Spaniards who set forth to discover and colonize America owed their allegiance not to each other but to the King and Queen of Spain. They were racially and religiously intolerant, scorned manual labor and were dedicated to accumulating riches through the efforts of those who were to be converted to Christianity. They were not motivated by the greater good of their people but by the pursuit of "gold, glory and God."[19] These explorers would later become the colonizers whose character and culture would serve as the imprint for the Cuban civilization.

The Spanish Empire.

Spain's overseas empire "dates from the joint rule of Isabella [I] of Castile and Ferdinand [V] of Aragon whose marriage in 1469 began the process of uniting the separate Iberian kingdoms into one Spanish nation."[20] Spanish exploration and conquest of the Americas was motivated by a desire to secure: "neighboring areas for defense against Muslim raids from North Africa,"[21] "shipping activities and trade in the Mediterranean Sea and Atlantic Ocean,"[22] and "neighboring areas as ports for export of gold and enslaved Africans."[23] They were also wanted to spread Christianity and increase trade with the Far East. In the area of trade, his majesties wanted to overcome the advantage the Portuguese had gained by establishing ports on the African continent and its surrounding islands.[24]

The Explorers

The year 1492 was a pivotal one for the Spanish Kingdom. In January of that year, his majesties completed the Christian Reconquest by defeating the Arabs and driving them from Spain. However, his majesties were concerned that Islam was advancing elsewhere posing a threat to the Spanish Kingdom. By 1502, the focus of the Inquisition shifted from Jews, to Arabs who had "insincerely converted to Christianity."[25] In order to pursue their Christian Crusades, his majesties supported Christopher Columbus who proposed to reach India or Asia by a westward route giving Spain an alternate passage to Muslim-held Jerusalem. They also hoped his voyage would bring Spain prestige and riches.[26] Thus, Spain justified its imperial expansion on four grounds: "to spread its religion [Christianity], to reinforce national unity and identity, to enhance Spain's international power, and to compete with Portugal for trade, territory and glory."[27]

During this period, it was common practice to take possession of un-chartered lands and their inhabitants. Pope Alexander VI who, in 1493, formally approved the division of the unexplored world between Spain and Portugal, validated this assumption based on the Spaniard's responsibility to spread Christianity to the inhabitants of the discovered lands. The Papal Decree was incorporated into the Treaty of Tordesillas (1494) that established the Line of Demarcation determining where the Spanish and Portuguese cultures would take root.[28]

The people who accompanied Columbus on his four voyages to the Americas were soldiers, officials of the Spanish Kingdom, priests, farmers, and African slaves. The majority did not intend to settle in the Americas. They relied on Indian and, later, slave labor for their sustenance and sought to find gold and return to Spain with riches. In this manner, the Spanish began to build their empire. Exploration gave way to conquest and, subsequently, colonization.

The Conquerors (Conquistadores)

Cuba attracted little attention from Spain until the Spanish colony on Hispaniola became overcrowded and indigenous labor grew scarce. In 1511, Diego Velasquez, a wealthy Spaniard residing on Hispaniola set sail for Cuba with over 300 Spanish soldiers.[29] He defeated the indigenous resistance led by Chief Hatuey and established the first permanent settlement on the island of Cuba. Future Spanish incursions resulted in the Indian's forced conversion to Catholicism and their subjugation to Spanish rule. By 1515, the Spanish conquerors had established many settlements.[30] The Spanish monarchs gave the conquerors and their soldiers "encomiendas" or "jurisdiction over geographic areas"[31] and the right to tax the indigenous population and to force them to work for the benefit of the landowner (encomendero). The landowners made the Indians (encomendados) work in mines, agricultural estates and as household servants. Many Indians were also sent to Spain to serve as soldiers. As a result of their displacement from the land and their social environment, as well as malnutrition, disease, and labor conditions, the Ciboney and the Arawaks were nearly annihilated by 1542. By 1555, the native population was estimated at 3,000.[32]

The Colonists

Once the Indians were conquered, the Monarchy appointed Diego Velasquez Governor of Cuba and established the political institutions through which they would govern the island until 1898. The governor possessed military powers accompanying the title of Captain-General and was responsible for running the government. The governor collected revenues and answered to the Tribunal of the Dominican Republic (Audencia of Santo Domingo). The Tribunal and the unannounced inspections performed by representatives of the Spanish Kingdom were the check-and-balance on the considerable powers of the governor. At the local level, the crown exercised control through the "Cabildo", a political, legal and administrative entity established in each settlement. The governor appointed the president of this body that was, by and large, responsible for the management of the settlement.[33]

This system developed to include an annual meeting of representatives from all "cabildos" during which a spokesman was selected to take colonial grievances forward to the Spanish crown. Unfortunately, opposition from the governor and interference from Spain crushed the fledgling effort to secure legitimate representation. By mid-sixteenth century, the system was beginning to implode as a result of balance of power disputes between the governor and the "cabildo" as well as among the "cabildo" members themselves. The autonomy of the "cabildo" was systematically curtailed by the Spanish crown through a series of measures designed to centralize power in the hands of the monarchy. To make matters worse, the crown instituted the practice of selling public office. In time, many of those who sought public office came to be those who were looking to make a comfortable living from the graft of public funds. This practice was to have a profound impact on the development of civil society and government in an independent Cuba.[34]

Cuba's importance diminished with the "discovery of gold in the American mainland and the conquest of the Aztec Empire in 1521."[35] The discovery of gold led many to leave Cuba and, in order to encourage the settlers to stay, the Spanish gave "encomiendas" "to single men and penalized those who left Cuba without permission."[36] Still, by 1550, Cuba's population was estimated at 700 Spaniards,[37] less than 5,000 Indians and a little fewer than 800 African slaves.[38]

A large part of the Spanish population actually consisted of Criollos who were not as well educated or culturally sophisticated as their ancestors. They were in a survival mode and, like their ancestors, lacking in patient effort. Corruption, violence and civil disobedience flourished. The church, which may have performed as a positive influence, became part of the problem. The crown appointed the ecclesiastical leadership in Cuba, which, for all practical purposes, served as an extension of the monarchy. Through a system of taxation, rents and donations the church amassed large amounts of land and wealth. By the seventeenth century, the church had abandoned its zeal to convert the "infidels" and was actively engaged in maintaining an environment in which it would continue to materially prosper at the expense of the poor. [39]

The African Slaves

Second only to the character of the Spanish explorer and conquistador, the African slave had the most significant influence on the development of the Cuban culture. The first slaves arrived in Cuba with the explorers and were primarily employed in the washing of gold. Later, toward the seventeenth century, Cuba began to import slaves to replace the rapidly disappearing Indians as laborers in copper mines and sugar plantations.[40] By 1650, African slaves numbered 5,000 compared to the Indian population of about 2,000.[41] The arrival of slaves resulted in one of the most notable characteristics of Latin American colonization.

Unlike the British and Dutch who colonized North America, the Latin American colonist co-habitated with the Indian natives and African slaves producing the first mestizos (half-breeds) and mulattoes (light skinned blacks). Some scholars cite this as the reason why Latin America exhibited and continues to exhibit greater racial tolerance than the US.[42] Beginning in the mid-1500s, the other European powers began to show interest in the wealth and natural resources Spain netted from her colonies in the Americas. The French were the first to invade Cuba in 1555 followed by the British beginning in the 1560s. The European powers increasingly engaged in colonization of the Caribbean and by the eighteenth century, British, French and Dutch incursions and colonization posed a serious threat to Spanish control.[43]

In the eighteenth century, world affairs would have a resounding impact on the Cuban economy and lead to dramatic changes in the demography and culture of the Cuban population. The first major event was the Seven Years War (1756-1763), which pitted France and Spain against the British. In 1762, Havana was attacked and held by the British for a period of ten months. During this ten-month period, Cuba was able to trade with England and its North American colonies and received large quantities of slaves thereby increasing its sugar production. Cuban landowners bought new land, additional sugar refineries, and imported unprecedented numbers of African slaves.[44]

Between 1780 and 1788, more than 18,000 slaves were taken to Cuba.[45] "Cuba's economy became a monoculture; "the economy boomed in years when world sugar prices were good and bust when prices went down."[46] The opening of trade also focused the attention of England and its colonies on Cuba as a source of raw material and a lucrative market for their exports. Likewise, Cubans developed a taste for Northern imports and an appreciation for potential Northern markets for its abundant natural resources. At the end of the war, when the British pulled out, Spain was forced to make concessions to appease the Cuban people in light of increasing European interest in Cuba.[47]

A second, and more significant event was the Haitian slave rebellion of 1791. When the rebellion broke out, Cuba was ready to step in to fill the void. Haiti's sugar production never matched its former output and Cuba emerged as the world's major sugar producer.[48] During this period, the sugar economy was irrevocably tied to slave labor. Thus, as sugar production increased, the slave trade gained momentum. Between 1811 and 1820, the decade of the greatest African slave trade, more than 161,000 African slaves were taken to Cuba.[49] By 1825, the black population in Cuba was greater than the white population.[50] This was of great concern to the white elite of the sugar plantations who feared a slave rebellion similar to Haiti's in 1790. Toward the last decade of the century, it is estimated there were 200,000 slaves working in sugar plantations.[51]

The life of the Cuban slave was harsh. Once a slave was put to work in a sugar field, his life expectancy shrank to eight years. He worked sixteen to nineteen hours per day from November to May and nine hours per day from June to October. Women could serve as field slaves and when they were, they worked the same hours as the men. Generally, slaves were well fed. Sundays and holidays were reserved for planting gardens for their subsistence and they could hold religious ceremonies during this time. A mixture of Catholicism and the African Lucumi religion emerged from the mix of the Spanish and African cultures. This religion, "Santeria" is still practiced by many Cubans on the island and in exile in the United States and abroad. Not all slaves accepted their plight. There were a few and some runaway slaves made it to the cities or interior mountain communities were they obtained their freedom. Under Cuban law, African slaves were also able to buy their freedom and their owners released some. Over time, this meant that Cuba, unlike the other colonies, had a large population of free blacks and mulattoes.[52]

According to the official census of 1774, the racial composition of the Cuban population was 56.4 percent white, 19.9 percent free blacks or mulattoes and 23.7 percent black slaves.[53] The population of free blacks worked as artisans, farmers, entrepreneurs, and professionals. During the eighteenth century, Cuba began to develop its own cultural and social institutions and slaves who had purchased their freedom formed association that paid for the education and medical treatment of its members. Some free blacks were able to advance into the middle class; however, most wealth continued to go to the Spaniards and Criollos.

Beginning in the latter part of the eighteenth century, the elite white were increasingly concerned that black intellectuals would incite emancipation and slave revolts. Cuba's monoculture was not yet ready to support the loss of slave labor; therefore, the issue of emancipation would weigh heavily on discussion of independence and annexation to the former British colonies. Emancipation came to the African slave in Cuba in 1886. In 1879, the Spanish crown had issued enacted a law abolishing slavery

11

via an eight year tutelage (patronato) that guaranteed the continued labor of blacks on the plantations in exchange for food, clothing and wages from their owners. Fortunately for the slaves, by 1886 sugar was developing into a more mechanized process that was not as labor intensive and it was cheaper for the plantation owner to hire freed blacks as laborers than to maintain them year round for a period of eight years. A related and equally important factor was the fact that the British abolished slavery in 1807 and were applying pressure on Spain to do the same. Additionally, the United States abolished slavery in 1808 dashing any hopes that annexation to the United States would sustain slavery in Cuba. Finally, an influx of Chinese and Indian laborers provided a cheap labor force unburdened by the moral yoke of slavery.[54]

Three Cultures, One People

Cuba's classes and races blended over thousands of years producing a mixture of religions, music, language, foods, architecture, and customs that combined the Indian, Spanish and African cultures into a new Cuban culture.[55] Fidel Castro was a product of this culture. He was born in 1926, the illegitimate child of a Spaniard and a household servant. Fidel Castro's father was an illiterate Spanish peasant who arrived in Cuba with nothing and died in 1956 leaving an estate of more than half a million dollars. He worked for the United Fruit Company in Cuba and it has been reported that he did not come upon his fortune in an entirely honest manner. Due to his father's good fortune, Fidel Castro was educated in exclusive Jesuit schools and received a law degree from the University of Havana.[56] Much has been written on Castro's character to identify the underlying reasons for his lust for power, revolutionary zeal, and unquestionable disdain for the United States.

The following part of this paper will not review the reasons for which Castro chose to take the path he took, but rather the reasons why the Cuban people so willingly allowed him to lead them on this path to self-destruction. In particular, the next part will examine the cultural factors that made it possible.

Notes

[1] Jaime Suchlicki, *Cuba from Columbus to Castro and Beyo*nd, 4th ed. (Brassey's Inc., 1997), 5.

[2] Fred Olson, *On the Trail of the Arawaks* (University of Oklahoma Press: Norman, 1974), 181.

[3] Suchlicki, *Columbus to Castro*, 5.

[4] Francine Jacobs, *The Tainos, The People Who Welcomed Columbus* (New York: J.P. Putnam's Sons, 1992), 16.

[5] Jacobs, 15.

[6] Suchlicki, *Columbus to Castro*, 8-9.

[7] Suchlicki, *Columbus to Castro*, 7-8.

[8] Jacobs, 25-28.

[9] Jacobs, 22-23.

[10] [K Lynn Stoner], Encarta 99 Encyclopedia, "Cuba," [CD ROM], (Microsoft Corporation, 1993-1998).

[11] Suchlicki, *Columbus to Castro,* 11.

[12] Mario Lazo, *American Foreign Policy Failures in Cuba: Dagger in the Heart*, (New York, New York: Twin Circle Publishing Company, 1968), 11.

[13] Lazo, 12.

[14] Lazo, 12.

[15] Encarta 99 Encyclopedia, "Spanish Empire," [CD ROM], (Microsoft Corporation, 1993-1998).

[16] Lazo, 12-13.

[17] Encarta 99 Encyclopedia, "Inquisition," [CD ROM], (Microsoft Corporation 1993-1998).

[18] Encarta 99 Encyclopedia, "Inquisition."

[19] Lazo, 13.

[20] Encarta 99 Encyclopedia, "Spanish Empire."

[21] Encarta 99 Encyclopedia, "Spanish Empire."

[22] Encarta 99 Encyclopedia, "Spanish Empire."

[23] Encarta 99 Encyclopedia, "Spanish Empire."

[24] Encarta 99 Encyclopedia, "Spanish Empire."

[25] Encarta 99 Encyclopedia, "Inquisition."

[26] Encarta 99 Encyclopedia, "Spanish Empire."

[27] Encarta 99 Encyclopedia, "Spanish Empire."

[28] Encarta 99 Encyclopedia, "Spanish Empire."

[29] [Stoner], "Cuba,"12.

[30] [Stoner], "Cuba," 12.

[31] [Stoner], Cuba,"13.

[32] [Stoner], Cuba,"13.

[33] Suchlicki, *Columbus to Castro*, 22-24.

[34] Suchlicki, *Columbus to Castro*, 23-24.

[35] [Stoner], "Cuba," 13.

[36] [Stoner], "Cuba," 13.

[37] [Stoner], "Cuba," 13.

Notes

[38] Suchlicki, *Columbus to Castro*, 28.

[39] Suchlicki, *Columbus to Castro*, 29.

[40] Scuhlicki, *Columbus to Castro*, 29-30.

[41] [Stoner], "Cuba," 14.

[42] Suchlicki, *Columbus to Castro*, 30-31.

[43] Suchlicki, *Columbus to Castro*, 32-40.

[44] [Stoner], "Cuba," 14.

[45] [Stoner], "Cuba," 16.

[46] [Stoner], "Cuba," 16.

[47] Suchlicki, *Columbus to Castro*, 44-45.

[48] [Stoner], "Cuba," 16.

[49] [Stoner], "Cuba," 16.

[50] Suchlicki, *Columbus to Castro*, 30.

[51] [Stoner], "Cuba," 16.

[52] [Stoner], "Cuba," 16-17.

[53] [Stoner], "Cuba," 17.

[54] Suchlicki, *Columbus to Castro*, 59-61.

[55] Suchlicki, *Columbus to Castro*, 59-61

[56] Lazo, 109-116.

PART II

CASTRO'S RISE TO POWER

How did a virtual unknown and political outsider manage to assume the pre-eminent leadership position in Cuba? More importantly, what was the allure for the Cuban people? This part will review the culture from which Cuban society emerged and the nurture under which it developed and show that, due to the nature of the Spanish colonization and the political and economic influence exerted by the US, the Cuban people were cultured and nurtured to accept Castro as the only alternative to a totalitarian government.

Of all the cultural elements inherited from the Spanish, the caliph mentality was, by far, the most critical and enduring from a political perspective. After seven centuries under Arab influence, the Spanish adopted the concept by establishing a monarchy with absolute control over civic and religious affairs.[1] Certainly there were those who believed the monarchy deceived its power from the people and, as such, should respect the rights of the people. However, the brave few who dared to oppose the monarchy would, at the very minimum, find themselves exiled. Interestingly, the fate of the Spanish and Cuban people may have been different if the Spanish monarchs had not banished the Jews from Spain following the Reconquest. That is, the Jews were at the time not only the intermediaries between the Spanish and the Arabs, but also Spain's emerging middle class. In their struggle to become a more substantial and representative body of socio-economic systems, the Jews would have increasingly sought to obtain the civil liberties that would have made Spain and, in turn, Cuba a more representative and democratic nation. However, religious fervor prevailed and the monarchial system under which Spain flourished crippled efforts to build a true democracy in an independent Cuba.[2]

By their actions, the Spanish monarchs created a culture based on totalitarianism, religious fanaticism, and racial intolerance. They produced nobles, soldiers, clergy, explorers, and conquerors who lacked the desire and experience to create viable political and fiscal systems within the territories they colonized. The totalitarian nature of the monarchy would also absolve the Spanish citizen from any social or civic responsibility and deprive him of the necessary tools to become an efficient leader or manager. The humanistic goal of bringing souls into the Christian community was in sharp contrast to the process of colonization whereby the Indians were exploited to extinction and Africans purchased into bondage. The Spaniards did not see a dichotomy between the exploitation of these populations and the tenets of Christianity. One of the reasons for this may have been that the Spanish considered the Indians and Africans inferior races destined to serve. The cultural legacy of their religious and, more importantly, their racial intolerance, surfaced as a contentious issue in the nineteenth century.[3]

For most of the nineteenth century, Cuba remained faithful to the "Mother Country". Although there were attempts made to rebel against the monarchy going as far back as 1809, they were sporadic and quickly disbanded. Generally, Cubans were in favor of working within the Spanish system and the limited reform movement called for free trade and political representation vis-à-vis Spain.[4] The independence movement gained momentum in the mid-nineteenth century leading to the Ten Years' War (1868-1878), the Little War (1879-1880), and the War of Independence (1895-1898). In 1898, Spain, which for three years had been unable to defeat the Cubans, offered to make Cuba a self-governing province. By then, the spirit of independence had taken root and the Cubans declined the offer.[5]

In its infancy, the United States, unable to deter European imperialistic expansion, opposed Cuban independence as it might upset the balance of power if the British or French were to move in. However, by the end of the nineteenth century, Spain had lost most of its empire and the United States was well in pursuit of its "Manifest Destiny." The Monroe Doctrine declared the United States would not look favorably upon a transfer of colonies from one European power to another[6] and the Spanish-Cuban situation had become a threat to the security of the United States. More importantly, the Spanish presence in the Western hemisphere was an impediment to economic expansion of the US.[7]

During the respective administrations, Presidents Polk, Pierce and Buchanan attempted to buy Cuba from Spain and in 1854, the Ostend Manifesto proposed to buy or forcibly take Cuba from Spain.[8] Less overt attempts were reported to have occurred during the presidencies of Taylor and Filmore by covert support to the Cuban annexationist movement.[9] Following the Ten Years' War, US investment in Cuba multiplied primarily via the purchase of sugar plantations and mining cites. Also, due to changes in the European market, the US also became Cuba's primary market for the sale of sugar.[10]

By 1898, when the US formally entered the Cuban scene by declaring war on Spain, Cuba's future, cast entirely from its ancestral nature and nurture, had been sealed. Those who fought so long and so hard for thirty years were not prepared to affect the course of events and the Cuban War of Independence became the Spanish-American War.

The US declared war on Spain on 25 April 1898. The Treaty of Paris by which Spain agreed to end its sovereignty to Cuba was signed on 10 December 1898.[11] The US government never accorded political recognition to the Cuban independence movement. Yet, the Cuban civilian leadership instructed its military leaders to place themselves under the command of the US forces and to secure their coastal landing.[12]

As a final affront to Cuban independence and the forces that had made a significant contribution to the US victory, the Cuban people were not represented at the Paris Peace Conference. In this manner, the descendants of a totalitarian political system supported by a monoculture economy missed the opportunity to forge a politically sovereign nation.[13] The leaders of the independence movement, being a product of their Spanish ancestry, were unable to resist the US' incursion into their economic and political existence. They had come to respect the North Americans who had themselves fought a war of independence from an imperialist power, established themselves as an enviable economic force, and fought a civil war that freed its African slaves.

Additionally, a segment of the population, primarily the business sector, preferred US military intervention to the turmoil of the thirty years during which they had been fighting for independence. Others may have accepted US military intervention and rule as a necessary, precursory step to defeat the Spanish and to create a stable political climate in which they could resume their economic endeavors. Irrespective of their position, they expected the US to withdraw from Cuba once the Cubans were capable of governing themselves.[14] Unfortunately, the "caliph mentality" failed the Cuban leaders of the independence movement. In effect, the principle of Manifest Destiny and the pursuit of economic expansion made Cuba a target of opportunity.

The Teller Amendment (20 April 1898) affirmed the US had no "intentions to exercise sovereignty, jurisdiction or control over said island except for the pacification thereof"[15] and the joint resolution giving President McKinley authority and power to intervene to end the hostility between Cuba and Spain clearly declared that upon termination of hostility, the US would leave the government and control of the island to its people."[16] However, in December of 1898, the Treaty of Paris made Cuba a trustee of the US which assumed the responsibility for the "protection life and property"[17] of Cuba.

Annexation was considered a possible solution to the "Cuban problem"; however, it was finally dismissed during the Paris Peace Conference because, the US realizing it would incur Cuba's war debt and liabilities of about $400 million, opted to seek other options that would support its economic and political control of Cuba.[18] In this manner, the US established a military government appointing General Brooke as its first military governor.

During his stewardship, General Brooke established a food distribution system and disbanded the Cuban army. His successor, General Wood, focused on improvements to the health and education systems. Under his administration, health facilities were constructed and the public school system was established.[19] He also had a profound impact on Cuba's political future. General Wood believed the people of Cuba were "a social element unworthy to be counted upon for collective purposes[20] and, in his opinion, they were "not ready for self government".[21] He proposed delegates be elected to frame a constitution and "as part [of the Constitutional Assembly], to provide for and agree with the government of the US [on] the relations to exist between that government and the government of Cuba."[22] In effect, he laid the foundation for the Platt Amendment.

From the Cuban perspective, the dawn of the twentieth century may be characterized as cautiously optimistic. The US occupation was generally viewed as a temporary condition and precursor to the development of a viable, autonomous republic. By 1901, it was clear to the US that its occupation of Cuba had to end; however, there was concern that once the US withdrew, it would loose all control and right of intervention.[23] While the Cuban Constitutional Convention was in session, the US Congress passed the Platt Amendment limiting Cuba's right to conduct its own foreign policy and granting the US the right to intervene in Cuba "for the maintenance of a government adequate for the protection of life, property and individual liberty."[24] The Amendment also leased land (Guantanamo) to the US to "maintain the independence of Cuba and to protect the people thereof, as well as its defense."[25]

There was considerable opposition to acceptance of the Amendment. General Juan Alberto Gomez' comment expressed the more nationalist sentiments, "The Platt Amendment has reduced the independence and sovereignty of the Cuban republic to a myth."[26] Others, preferred a limited independence to the US' continued military presence. The outcome was not surprising. The US position was quite clear; if the convention refused to accept the Platt Amendment as part of the Constitution, the US would not withdraw from Cuba and would not authorize an electoral law, elections or adoption of the new constitution. In the face of these alternatives, the convention

21

delegates adopted the Amendment by a vote of fifteen to fourteen[27] as an amendment to the Cuban Constitution of 1901. The Platt Amendment had significant impact on Cuba's socio-political development.

In December of 1901, Cuba held its first presidential elections. The electorate excluded Afro-Cubans, and men and women with less than $250 worth of assets. The elected president was Tomas Estrada Palma, of the Revolutionary Party. During his presidency, the US and Cuba signed the commercial reciprocity treaty that solidified US control of the Cuban economic market. Also, under the right-to-lease-land proviso of the Platt Amendment, the US was given sovereignty over Guantanamo Bay. Although the US and Cuba abrogated the Platt Amendment in 1934, the naval base at Guantanamo remains controversial and undoubtedly surface as a transition issue for a post-Castro Cuba. [28]

The new republic did not experience major social upheavals of race, class or religion. The economy was increasingly dependent on the US; however, it continued to develop. Its first years were marked by continued improvement in public health and education programs.[29] Conversely, Spanish culture and nurture continued to have a negative influence on the development of Cuba's socio-economic systems. The US inadvertently supported the "caliph" mentality" by absolving the Cubans from political responsibility via the Platt Amendment. The Cubans knew they could rely on the US to protect them from external threats or domestic conflict and failed to develop a true democratic government.[30]

The establishment of a republic and an electoral process did not guarantee a democracy. Toward the end of the first decade of the republic, electoral fraud, corruption, and the use of public office to amass personal wealth flourished in the new republic. There was growing disillusionment and pessimism especially among political leaders, intellectuals and students. As conditions worsened, there was an increased tendency to resolve political and economic problems through violent means Unfortunately, the inefficiency of the government was left unchecked for the republic lacked a civil society educated in the process of democratic self-government.[31]

From 1906 to 1917, Cuba elected three presidents, Tomas Estrada Palma (1902-1906), Jose Miguel Gomez (1909-1913) and Mario Garcia Menocal (1913-1921).[32] On three separate occasions, the US, under the provisions of the Platt Amendment, sent troops and ships to Cuba to quell uprisings led by groups attempting to overthrow the government accusing the incumbent leaders of corruption and ruthlessness.[33] The first US post-independence intervention occurred in 1906, when President Estrada manipulated elections in order to remain in power and an insurrection ensued leading Palma to request US intervention. President Theodore Roosevelt sent William Howard Taft, who was, at the time, the Secretary of War, to assess the situation. Facing overwhelming opposition, Palma was persuaded to resign and Taft appointed himself Provisional Governor of Cuba. He served for nearly thirty days and was succeeded by Charles E. Magoon.

The provisional governments of Taft and Magoon were in place from 1906 to 1909. The Magoon administration encouraged the proliferation of patronage in appointment to public office and increased spending creating a national deficit.[34] However, his provisional government also "drew up an organic body of law for the executive and judiciary, and for provisional and municipal government."[35] Equally important were the electoral laws that led to the US' decision to call for elections in 1909.[36]

The US government was confident the new electoral laws would facilitate legitimate elections and, in 1909, Magoon relinquished his position to the newly elected Jose Miguel Gomez (Liberal, 1909-1913). During the Gomez administration, racial relations, which had never been a political issue, deteriorated. When the Cuban Senate passed the Moura Law banning the creation of parties based on race, [37] the Independent Color Association, dedicated to increasing political opportunities for Afro-Cubans, organized an uprising in 1912. The uprising, led by a veteran of the War of Independence was quickly crushed when President Taft sent the battleship Nebraska to Havana, deployed support forces to Key West, Florida and landed Marines in Daiquiri, Cuba.[38]

Mario Garcia Menocal (Conservative) was elected president in 1913.[39] His re-election in 1916 sparked the last US intervention of this period. The Liberal Party, led by former President Gomez, protested the fraudulent re-election of President Menocal. The US supported President Menocal, provided weapons and ammunition and landed about 500 Marines throughout the island.[40] This enabled President Menocal to consolidate his forces and defeat the rebels. During the Menocal administration, Cuba joined the Allies in World War I and emerged as a major world sugar supplier.[41]

Cuba elected two more presidents between 1921 and 1932. Alfredo Zayas (1921-1924) and Gerardo Machado (1924-1932). During this 13-year period, insurrections continued led by various Cuban groups opposed to the ongoing corruption in government. "Disregard for educational matters served to aggravate an already precarious situation"[42] as there was a "divorce between education and the island's real needs [perpetuated by] the old Spanish attitude that favored intellectual over manual labor."[43] Many Cubans continued to show disdain for manual labor opting to pursue careers in law and medicine which they preferred to practice in Havana. Therefore, the agrarian and rural populations lacked services available in the cities and the urban population suffered from high unemployment or underemployment. The university students were among those who were increasingly disillusioned because they were unable to find suitable employment and lacked intellectual challenges. They became an increasingly visible and vociferous medium for radical change.

In 1920, Cuba entered a period of economic crisis after a drop in sugar prices that led many to question the nature of the economic relationship that existed between the US and Cuba. The resulting economic nationalism led to an "anti-US feeling; xenophobia, and the retrieval of the national wealth became the main themes of this blossoming nationalism."[44] As the economic crisis deepened, Cuba was preparing for presidential elections. Alfredo Zayas (Conservative) who ran against the former President Jose Miguel Gomez supporters employed amnestied criminals and murderers to intimidate voters. The US responded by sending General Enoch Crowder to Cuba to supervise new elections, which he proceeded to do from aboard the battleship Minnesota.[45] Alfredo Zayas was elected in 1920. His tenure (1921-1924) was marked by graft and inefficiency.

Following the election, Crowder used US officials to inspect several branches of the Cuban government resulting in the resignation of the Cuban cabinet. Crowder replaced the cabinet with his own "Honest Cabinet" composed of a number of distinguished Cubans. The "Honest Cabinet" reduced the budget, trimmed the bureaucracy and annulled several public works contracts [that] would have enriched a number of public servants."[46] Much to his credit, Zayas was able to conclude financial assistance and trade agreements ameliorating the national deficit. However, the economic nationalism and social reform movements were fueled y US intervention in Cuban political and economic affairs and "the failure to achieve the needed reforms, thrust upon the university students….the leadership of the brewing revolution."[47] President Zayas, emboldened by rising Cuban nationalism and foreign loans, contributed to Cuba's effort to assert its sovereignty by disbanding the "Honest Cabinet".[48]

Machado (Liberal, 1924-1928 and 1929-1932) campaigned against the corruptions of the Zayas administration. He promised reforms in social services, the army, and education. Once he was elected in 1924, he proceeded to subjugate the other political parties and those he could not influence or bribe were imprisoned or deported. He closed bars and gambling establishments and created a censorship board. However, he did little to curtail government corruption and did not, as promised, take steps to abrogate the Platt Amendment.[49]

Meanwhile, Cuban students inspired by the Spanish anarcho-syndicalist movement of the nineteenth century, the Mexican Revolution, and the Bolshevick Revolution in Russia, the students began to explore solutions to Cuba's problems.[50] The Cardoba Reform movement in Argentina, which made the university there a focal point of national reform, was especially appealing to Cuba's university students who sought academic and administrative reforms that would make the university an active, if not leading participant, in the national reform movement. In 1923, Julio Antonio Mella, a law student with strong anti-American convictions, organized the First Congress of Cuban

Students. Later, he collaborated with Mexican Communists in gathering all of Cuba's communist groups for an island-wide conference in 1925. This Congress was the precursor to Cuba's Communist Party.[51]

During this period, disillusionment and frustration continued to nurture feelings of nationalism or "Cubanismo" and a quest to find options to a monoculture economy that failed to provide for the economic prosperity of its people.[52] There was also a growing anti-American feeling rising from continued economic and political dependence to the US.

Although he'd pledged not to run a second term, Machado obtained an amendment from the Constitutional Convention that extended his tenure. In November of 1928, via a fraudulent election in which he ran unopposed, Machado was elected to a new six-year term (1929-1935). Machado's second term coincided with the Great Depression and a collapse in the price of sugar. The ensuing economic crisis coupled with political unrest, led him to adopt increasingly repressive measures. Student militancy grew as did their prestige and support.

The "Generation of 1930" as the students came to be called, sponsored many demonstrations. In 1930, the Machado regime responded by expelling students then closing the University of Havana. The University closure actually exacerbated matters. The students responded by forming more radical and militant organizations such as the University Student Directory and the Student Left Wing. Eventually members of the student left wing became part of the Cuban Communist Party and the ABC, a terrorist cell that opposed both the Student Directory and Student Left Wing.[53]

When the political chaos began to take its toll on Cuban-American business interests, the "Platt Amendment" or "caliph" mentality kicked in. The voices of Cubans, who desired political stability and the accompanying economic prosperity, overwhelmed that of the students, writers and intellectuals pursuing "Cubanismo" and reform. Toward the latter part of 1933, Sumner Wells was sent to Cuba as a special envoy to mediate between Machado and the opposition. The mediation was highly criticized by opposition groups and general strikes ensued. Machado's repressive machine failed to restore order and Wells was convinced the solution was for Machado to resign. Even the army, which had been generally supportive, rose up against the regime when it became evident the increasing rift between Machado and Wells might result in US military intervention. With the country on the verge of revolution, facing a general strike, defection of the military and possible US military intervention to depose him, Machado resigned and left Cuba in August of 1933. Wells recommended Carlos Manuel Cespedes, the son of Cuba's first president and former Cuban Ambassador to Washington, to assume the position of provisional president (August 1933-September 1933).[54]

Cespedes encountered significant opposition from Cuban reformists, especially the students, who believed the new regime was a tool of the US and that it was intent on slowing down the reform movement. They interpreted Cespedes' reinstatement of the 1901 Constitution, which mirrored the US Constitution, as a sign of his pro-US position. The political climate was increasingly anti-American, non-interventionist and focused on the issues of social and economic justice commonly expressed by the Communists.

The "Machadato," or overthrow of Machado, signaled "the beginning of an era of reform"[55]. The revolutionary wave that swept away the dictatorship had begun to acquire the characteristics of a major revolution"[56] with the Generation of 1930 at the helm of the revisionist agenda. The provisional government was short-lived and the elections projected for February of 1934 would never take place.

In September of 1933, enlisted members of the Army, who faced a reduction in pay and restriction of promotion, met with officers to discuss their grievances. The officers refused to negotiate leaving the camp in control of the enlisted men. A group of university students, hoping to capitalize on the event, met with the soldiers and managed to convert an act of military "insubordination into a full-fledged military coup able to serve revolutionary ends."[57] Those who took part in the "Sergeants' Revolt," led by Sergeant-stenographer Fulgencio Batista, had nothing to loose as they faced administrative punishment due to their insubordination.[58]

The student Directorio, with the assistance of the military participants, pounced on the opportunity to establish a government without US intervention and forced Cepedes to relinquish the presidency to a five-man coalition. The US did not recognize the coalition government and although President Roosevelt was not inclined to intervene, a fleet of navel vessels was sent to Cuba. Several factors contributed to the collapse of the coalition to include their decision to nominate a candidate for the presidency that did not have Directorio support. The Directorio removed the coalition government appointed Ramon Grau San Martin, a former professor at the University of Havana who had supported the Directorio, provisional president (September 10 1933 to January 15,1934).[59]

The self-appointed Colonel Batista did not support the Directorio's action. Moreover, the US did not recognize the Grau government and was increasingly alarmed by the regime's political agenda. In less than four months, Grau abrogated the 1901 Constitution, asked for the abrogation of the Platt Amendment, and implemented an ambitious reform program focused on improving conditions for the labor force. His labor organization and nationalization laws intended to increase the rights and benefits of the Cuban worker and to limit competition or influence. Several of these laws aimed at "Cubanizing" the labor movement increasing the number of Cubans in the workforce (vice Spaniards) and improving the benefits of the Cuban worker.[60]

US opposition grew with "Grau's seizure of two American-owned sugar mills…and his temporary take-over of the Cuban Electric Company."[61] The US continual refusal to recognize the government created problems for Grau particularly with Cuban political and business leaders who considered US recognition a necessity for continued political stability and economic prosperity. In lieu of recognition, the US encouraged opposition from the Communists, the displaced army officers, and the ABC who were, not surprisingly, at odds each other as well. This inner conflict, opposition from business leaders and Grau's inability to negotiate or impose a solution, led to the collapse of his government.[62]

In October of 1933, Welles met with Batista to assure him he [Batista] had the power and support to restore order and to keep Cuba from the disaster that would accompany the imminent collapse of the Grau government. On January 14, 1934, Batista forced Grau to resign. He proceeded to install three presidents: Carlos Hevia (3 days), Manuel Marquez Sterling y Guiral (less than one day) and Colonel Carlos Mendieta. Mendieta, (January 1934–1935), was recognized by the US. However, Batista was in complete control of Cuban affairs.[63] Batista's actions "had a profound impact on subsequent

Cuban developments and events. Moreover, these events gave university students a sense of power and catapulted them into the mainstream of politics [creating] an awareness among the students and the population at large of the need as well as the possibility rapid and drastic change."[64]

During the Mendieta administration, Cuba and the US signed the Treaty of Relations that abrogated the Permanent Treaty of 1903 and the Platt Amendment. A new Reciprocity Treaty was also signed covering mutual tariff reductions. However, those who thought the end of the Machado administration marked a re-dedication to government reform, were disillusioned. Government corruption continued and repression and terrorism were on the rise. The students who decided to pursue revolutionary ideals formed the Autentico Party in 1934. The new party was a nationalist forum for social and civil liberties as well as economic reform. Joven Cuba was also founded during this period and employed urban violence as a means to reform Cuba's polity and society. These groups were particularly active during the Mendieta regime. The University opened in 1934 giving the students a forum to vent their frustrations and a platform for the civil demonstrations that followed.

Between 1934 and 1935 there were approximately one hundred strikes. A general strike organized by the students in 1935 was broken in a matter of days. Government repression escalated and the university was again closed. Omnipotent military control and the use of military firing squads to execute civilians took their toll on public support. Mendieta resigned in 1935 failing to arrive at a negotiation between the political parties in preparation for the 1936 elections. Batista continued to exhert influence through the administrations of Jose A. Barnet (Provisional 1935-1936), Miguel Mariano Gomez (1936), and Federico Laredo Bur (1936-1940).[65]

During this period, Batista supported public works projects and education extending schools to rural areas where they had been non-existent. However, he continued to show signs of a dictatorship mentality and propensity to circumvent the electoral process. In 1936, President Gomez, in an attempt to re-assert civilian control, dismissed thousands of military reservists from public office and vetoed a nine-cent sugar tax proposed by Batista for a program whereby army sergeants would be sent to rural areas to teach in newly elected schools. This placed the President in direct and final conflict with Batista. Lacking public and congressional support, Gomez was impeached by a Senate trial that many believe was instigated by Batista.[66]

Ever true to their Spanish culture and nurture, in 1936 most Cubans saw Batista as a strong man who brought Cuba order and stability. Initially he was respected for his ability to get things done.[67] Later, the issue of how he got things done, would become more relevant. Also, due to highly successful repressive measures, student opposition was almost non-existent following the failure of the general strike in 1935. In 1940, Cuba adopted a new Constitution that included, among other civil liberties, universal suffrage.[68]

Batista was the first president elected under the new Constitution beating his closest opponent by 300,000 votes.[69] When the Second World War broke out, Batista sided with the US declaring war on the Axis Powers in 1941. As an emergency war measure, the Cuban Congress gave Batista, among other powers, the authority to impose taxes, regulate labor, and enter into military pacts with the US. Within days, Batista raised

taxes and created new ones including the island's first income tax.[70] He also made a deal

with the US to sell sugar at about two cents per pound at a great sacrifice to the Cuban

economy.[71]

In order to complete emergency construction projects and to support defense plans,

labor law restrictions were lifted. Tax exemptions were granted representing millions of

dollars of savings to the US at a loss to Cuba.[72] These war measures coupled with a

shortage of consumer goods incurred discontent among the Cuban population.

Nevertheless, Batista enjoyed the support of the upper as well as the labor classes. In

1943, he also received Communist support and legalized the Communist Party, which

changed its name to Partido Socialista Popular or Popular Socialist Party (PSP).[73]

In 1944, Grau San Martin returned defeating Batista's chosen successor by a good

majority. The Grau administration (1944-1948) has been labeled "the most incompetent

and corrupt in Cuban history."[74] Labor unrest increased with rising conflict between

communist and non-communist organizations.[75] Graft and political patronage reached an

all time high with Grau himself accused of misappropriation of $174 million.[76] In the

social context, Grau failed to curtail political corruption and organized violence. The

university provided refuge to criminals and student politics enveloped the organized use

of force.

The Autentico's failure to bring order to chaos, created a split in the party. Eduardo

Chibas broke form the party forming the Ortodoxo Party in 1947. Chibas was a member

of the 1930 Generation and symbolized the ideals of the reform movement that began in the 1920s. Fidel Castro, at the time, a high school student, idolized Chibas who had a Sunday radio program during which he criticized government corruption and honesty in public office. The students felt the nationalistic platform of Chiba's Ortodoxo Party rekindled ideals abandoned by the Communist and Autentico parties. Many Cubans enthusiastically supported Chibas and believed he represented Cuba's best and brightest hope for saving its political system and establishing true sovereignty. In 1951, following one of his radio addresses, Chibas shot himself. His criticism of the Autentico Party had practically destroyed it and the Communist Party lacked support particularly from the students who believed the Communists had been too conciliatory of past regimes. Without Chibas, the Ortodoxo Party lacked a charismatic leader.[77]

Carlos Prio (1948– 952) made limited strides in curbing organized crime activity; however, his administration was as corrupt as Grau's. On the economic front, Cuba experienced rapid economic growth in the years following the Second World War. Cuba's sugar industry expanded as a result of the waning European and Asian markets and sugar prices rose by 40%. During the war years, Cuba was able to amass a large amount of foreign exchange; however it was scarcely used toward economic diversification.[78] The "Cubanization" efforts of the 1930s increased the number of Cuban-owned sugar mills from 54 in 1939 to 113 in 1952.[79] However, further economic development was hampered by the fact that Cuba was still too dependent on sugar production for revenue. Cuba also suffered from unemployment, underemployment and economic disparity between rural and urban populations. Unemployment and underemployment rose to 17 and 13 percent respectively between 1956 and 1957. The economicdisparity disparity between urban and rural populations grew and the rural illiteracy rate was almost four times higher in rural areas.[80]

It was under these conditions that Cuba prepared for its 1952 election. On March 10, 1952, Batista, realizing that he would not win the elections, staged a successful coup. Under the auspices of restoring order, Batista cancelled the election, suspended the 1940 Constitution and became Cuba's first dictator. His actions destroyed all hope of building a viable constitutional democracy. The coup was tolerated by a society that had never developed truly democratic institutions. The executive, legislative and judicial branches lacked the necessary autonomy or checks and balances. The army had not been trained to perform as a professional organization subservient to civilian control. Batista's promise to allow elections in 1953 also contributed to the acceptance of the population. As expected, the business community welcomed the stability imposed by his quick and decisive take-over. [81]

Batista's return to power was great for business. The mining and tourist industries benefited as did neglected public works projects. He made low cost housing available and built a water system in Havana. Batista ruled the government through force and, as he increased the use of force to maintain order and control, his political base narrowed. The entrepreneurs remained steadfast supporters; however, large segments of the population opposed continued military control. A malaise spread among the writers, intellectuals and students and the government's censorship led to increased violence and terrorist activity. Once again, the university students spread the evolutionary zeal in the safe-haven of the campus and were free to plot against the government. Fidel Castro, a

1950 graduate of the University of Havana Law School, was one of the followers of Chibas' Ortodoxo Party.[82]

In July 26, 1953, Castro his brother, Raul, and a group of revolutionaries attacked the Moncada Barracks disguising the move as an Ortodoxo uprising supported by pro-Ortodoxo army officers. Due to the celebration of a local festival, Castro expected a decreased state of readiness and hoped to confuse the army elements keeping them from taking up arms in support of the Batista regime. Poor planning and lack of communication resulted in a complete fiasco. Castro and his brother were captured and jailed. During his trial, he presents "History Will Absolve Me" as his defense and declared his reform movement was in line with the ideals expressed by Marti and Chibas and in line with Cuban tradition.[83] Likewise, in the "Moncada Manifesto", which he had intended to read if the assault had succeeded, Castro failed to make mention of a Marxist-Leninist agenda.[84] In fact, in 1953, the Cuban Communist Party had no political power base and had lost its credibility when it aligned itself with Machado and Batista.[85]

In 1954, when Batista was elected unopposed via fraudulent election, Cuban leaders tried in vain to convince him to hold new elections. Failure to reach compromise resulted in riots that lasted for months. In May of 1955, Batista granted amnesty to Castro and his followers. Castro left Cuba shortly after his release. While in Mexico, Castro met Che Guevara with whom he collaborated in organizing the July 26 Movement named in commemoration of Castro's attack of the Moncada Barracks in 1953. Of the eighty-two men who accompanied Castro on his return to Cuba on board the Granma in December of 1956, approximately 24 were killed in the first encounter with the Batista forces. Those who were not killed or who did not abandon the cause established a base in the Sierra Maestra Mountains.[86]

Again, as he had done following the attack on the Moncada Barracks, Castro was able to convince the remaining eleven men that they had triumphed in the first stage of the revolution and that victory would ultimately be theirs.[87]   Meanwhile, student opposition strengthened with the closure of the University of Havana in 1956 (the university opened again in 1959).   Many joined terrorist organizations that focused, not on government reform and social development, but on the overthrow of the Batista regime.[88]   In January of 1957, Castro's revolutionary army amounted to approximately eighteen men. The 26 July Movement would have died a natural death if it were not for four factors: the Herbert L. Matthews articles, the urban revolutionary cells, Batista's excessive retaliatory measures and the US weapons embargo.[89]

Herbert L. Matthews entered the picture in 1957 when, at Castro's bequest, he was chosen by the New York Times to interview Castro in the Sierra Maestra Mountains. Castro was looking for a reporter who would be able to tell his story and, from his perspective Matthews was the perfect choice.   Matthews had not only been openly critical of the Batista regime, but also could give Castro access to the audience he needed to reach in order to influence public opinion and affect political change – the US. In his first article, Matthews wrote the 26 July Movement, "amounts to a new deal for Cuba, radical democratic and therefore anti-communist."[90] He described Castro as "a man of ideals" [of] "liberty, democracy, social justice, the need to restore the Constitution and hold elections."[91]   In his second article, he assured his readers "there [was] no Communism to speak of in Fidel Castro's 26th of July Movement."[92] Matthews' articles

37

opened the floodgates for American journalists into the Sierra Maestra. By the summer

of 1957, Castro was a regular on US network news and numerous articles and books were

written on Castro's idealistic quest.[93]

The 26 July Movement grew in prestige and gained momentum from the favorable

press and the simple fact that it and its leader continued to survive opposed by an army of

over 20,000 men.[94] Rural guerrilla warfare spread to urban centers where students,

members of the Directorate, Autentico Party and other factions allied themselves to the

movement and undermined the regime through acts of terrorism. By the end of 1957,

Castro's forces had increased to fewer than 100 men organized into mobile units

proficient in guerrilla warfare.[95] The fact that Batista's forces were unable to defeat them

increased the prestige of the revolutionary movement to the detriment of the armed

forces. Increasing urban terrorist activity resulted in extreme retaliatory government

action and public display of the tortured bodies of real or suspected revolutionaries.[96]

The US' support of the Batista regime began to wane toward the latter part of 1957.

Castro's positive press and charisma appealed to the liberal sector of the American

population. Conversely, Batista's repressive tactics alienated even those who opposed

Castro and his guerrilla movement. On 14 March 1958, under increasing pressure to

withdraw support from Batista, the US declared an arms embargo against the Batista

regime.[97] Additionally, the US State Department began to question Cuba's use of the

equipment purchased under the Military Defense Assistance Program emphasizing its use

was to be limited to hemispheric defense with the approval of the US. These actions

made it difficult for the armed forces to mount an attack or defense. They also had a

profound psychological impact in that they were interpreted as a signal the US had withdrawn its support of Batista in favor of Castro.[98]   Reportedly, there were other options discussed and rejected by the US. Among them, the Catholic Church proposed a "government of unity"[99] derived from mediation between Batista and Castro.   A "caretaker government"[100] composed of all political groups was also proposed as a precursor to elections supervised by the United Nations.

Meanwhile, the presidential elections regularly scheduled for June of 1958 were postponed to November. The request for United Nations observers was not answered in time and the government-sponsored candidate won in what was generally assessed as a fraudulent election. At this point, Cubans, like their North American neighbors, came to believe they had only one choice – Castro. On December 9, 1958, William D. Pawley, an emissary of the Eisenhower administration, was sent to Cuba to try to persuade Batista to accept exile in Florida leaving a caretaker government in place to be followed by elections within eighteen months. It is not clear whether Batista refused to accept Pawley's proposal because he was intent on his candidate assuming office or because he failed to understand Pawley's plan had the support of President Eisenhower. Regardless, Pawley failed in his attempt to keep Castro from being the only alternative. Within days, Batista was notified he could no longer count on the support of the US and, on January 1, 1959, Batista left Cuba.[101]

Initially, Castro did not assume a leadership position in the new government. He assumed the position of Commander of the Armed Forces and appointed Manuel Urrutia president. The United States recognized the new Cuban government on January 7, 1959 and, on January 8, 1959, Castro marched into Havana.[102] Castro, who is credited with a charismatic personality, enviable intellect and superb oratory skills spoke the words

Cubans longed to hear and was hailed as the new messiah. He chastised a corrupt government and society and promised needed changes. Undoubtedly, in the eyes of the Cubans and those in the United States who were still in a position to influence Cuban political affairs, Castro would cure the malaise permeating Cuba and the one to restore the stability that would enable business to continue to flourish. In February of 1957, the new Cuban government passed the Fundamental Law of the Republic reinstating and modifying the 1940 Constitution. When the Prime Minister resigned in protest to Castro's autocratic decision to vest legislative power in the cabinet, Castro assumed the position of Prime Minister.[103]

Soon after, a rift developed between President Urrutia and Castro who felt Urrutia should be content to be a figurehead. Urrutia resigned in July of 1959 and Castro appointed Osvaldo Dorticos (Communist) the new president.[104] Dorticos served as president for almost 18 years as Castro did not appoint himself president until December 3, 1976. Under the 1976 Constitution, the offices of the President and Prime Minister were combined and the President of Cuba now serves as the head of state, head of government and commander-in-chief of the armed forces.[105]

At this point, it is important to emphasize that one of the major tenets of the "Declaration of the Sierra Maestra" was a demand for general elections under the terms of the 1940 Constitution.[106] Therefore, in order to remain in power, Castro had to find a way to circumvent the goal of the revolution (political and government reform) and to focus on a social agenda that included land, educational, tariff and wage reforms. To this end, in March of 1959, Castro nationalized the Cuban telephone company and reduced telephone rates. In April, he adopted the Agrarian Reform Law putting a limit on private land holdings with the state expropriating the remainder. The land reform law had the support of the majority of the Cuban people; however, it had been drawn up without public participation. These measures were viewed with concern by those who were critical of the autocratic means by which they were adopted and those who believed they represented communist encroachment.[107]

Castro's doctrine of "humanism" complimented his diversionary tactics. "Humanism" was to guarantee food to the people without the volatility of the capitalist system of supply and demand. It would also provide for the needy in lieu of subjugation to communism. "Humanism" would not take Cuba left or right, but forward.[108] Thus, Castro was able to divert not only the attention of the Cuban people, but also the world.

Notes

[1] Lazo, 12.

[2] Lazo, 11.

[3] Lazo, 11-16.

[4] Suchlicki, *Columbus to Castro,* 64-65.

[5] Suchlicki, *Columbus to Castro,* 48.

[6] *Monroe Doctrine; December 2, 1823* [document on-line], (The Avalon Project at Yale Law School, 1999, accessed on February 27, 2000); available from Internet http://www.yale.edu/lawweb/avalon/diplomacy/sp1898.htm; Internet.

[7] Geoff Simons, *Cuba from Conquistador to Castro* (New York: St Martin's Press, 1996), 85-197.

[8] [Stoner], *"Cuba,"* 18.

[9] Suchlicki, *Columbus to Castro,* 48.

[10] Suchlicki, *Columbus to Castro,* 48.

[11] Simons, 194.

[12] Simons, 202.

[13] Simons, 203-204.

[14] Suchlicki, *Columbus to Castro,* 80-82.

[15] Simons, 193.

[16] Simons, 193

[17] *The Treaty of Peace Between the United States and Spain* [document on-line], (The Avalon Project at Yale Law School, 1999, accessed on February 27, 2000.); available from http://www.yale.edu/lawweb/avalon/monroe.htm; Internet

[18] Simons, 204.

[19] Simons, 204-212.

[20] Simons, 207.

[21] Simons, 207.

[22] Simons, 208.

[23] Simons, 208.

[24] *The Platt Amendmet;* extract printed in Geoffrey Simons, *Cuba from Conquistador to Castro* (New York: St Martin's Press, 1996), 212.

[25] *The Platt Amendment;* extract printed in Geoffrey Simons, *Cuba from Conquistador to Castro* (New York: St Martin's Press, 1996), 212.

[26] Juan Alberto Gomez; quoted in Geoff Simons, *Cuba from Conquistador to Castro* (New York: St Martin's Press, 1996), 212.

[27] Simons, 211.

[28] Simons, 212-213.

[29] Suchlicki, *Columbus to Castro,* 87-88.

[30] Suchlicki, *Columbus to Castro,* 88.

[31] Suchlicki, *Columbus to Castro,* 88-90.

[32] Simons, 213-222.

[33] Simons, 213-222.

[34] Suchlicki, *Columbus to Castro,* 90.

[35] Suchlicki, *Columbus to Castro,* 90.

[36] Suchlicki, *Columbus to Castro,* 90.

Notes

[37] [Stoner], *Cuba*, 26.

[38] Simons, 218.

[39] Simons, 219.

[40] Simons, 219.

[41] Suchlicki, *Columbus to Castro*, 91.

[42] Suchlicki, *Columbus to Castro*, 91.

[43] Suchlicki, *Columbus to Castro*, 92.

[44] Suchlicki, *Columbus to Castro*, 93.

[45] Simons, 227.

[46] Suchlicki, *Columbus to Castro*, 93.

[47] Suchlicki, *Columbus to Castro*, 94-95.

[48] Suchlicki, *Columbus to Castro*, 94-95.

[49] Simons, 235-236.

[50] Simons, 238-244.

[51] Suchlicki, *Columbus to Castro*, 96-98.

[52] Suchlicki, *Columbus to Castro*, 95-96.

[53] Suchlicki, *Columbus to Castro*, 100-104.

[54] Suchlicki, *Columbus to Castro*, 105-107.

[55] Suchlicki, *Columbus to Castro*, 108.

[56] Suchlicki, *Columbus to Castro*, 108.

[57] Simons, 250.

[58] Simons, 250.

[59] Simons, 250-252.

[60] Simons, 252-254.

[61] Suchlicki, *Columbus to Castro*, 112.

[62] Suchlicki, *Columbus to Castro*, 113.

[63] Simons, 254-255.

[64] Suchlicki, *Columbus to Castro*, 117.

[65] Suchlicki, *Columbus to Castro*, 116-118.

[66] Lazo, 68.

[67] Lazo, 69-70.

[68] Suchlicki, *Columbus to Castro*, 119-120.

[69] Simons, 256.

[70] Lazo, 76.

[71] Suchlicki, *Columbus to Castro*, 120-121.

[72] Lazo, 78.

[73] Suchlicki, *Columbus to Castro*, 121.

[74] Lazo, 80.

[75] Lazo, 81.

[76] Simons, 257.

[77] Suchlicki, *Columbus to Castro*, 125-131.

[78] [Stoner], *Cuba*, 34.

[79] Suchlicki, *Columbus to Castro*, 134.

[80] Suchlicki, *Columbus to Castro*, 135-136.

Notes

[81] Lazo, 88-92.

[82] Lazo, 88-92.

[83] Suchlicki, *Columbus to Castro,* 138-142.

[84] *"Manifesto and Programme of 26 July Movement (November 1956)"*; extract printed in Geoffrey Simons, *Cuba from Conquistador to Castro* (New York: St Martin's Press, 1996), 362.

[85] Suchlicki, *Columbus to Castro,* 107.

[86] Simons, 277.

[87] Lazo, 121.

[88] Suchlicki, *Columbus to Castro,* 147.

[89] Lazo, 121-186.

[90] Herbert L. Matthews, The New York Times, February 24, 1957. Quoted in Mario Lazo, *American Policy Failures in Cuba Dagger in the Heart* (New York, New York: Twin Circle Publishing, 1968), 125.

[91] Herbert L. Matthews, The New York Times, February 24, 1957. Quoted in Mario Lazo, *American Policy Failures in Cuba Dagger in the Heart (*New York, New York: Twin Circle Publishing, 1968), 125.

[92] Herbert L. Matthews, The New York Times, February 24, 1957. Quoted in Mario Lazo, *American Policy Failures in Cuba Dagger in the Heart* (New York, New York: Twin Circle Publishing, 1968), 125.

[93] Lazo, 128-130.

[94] Simons, 284.

[95] Lazo, 135.

[96] Suchlicki, *Columbus to Castro,* 151.

[97] Suchlicki, *Columbus to Castro,* 151-152.

[98] Lazo, 159-164.

[99] Lazo, 166.

[100] Lazo, 167.

[101] Lazo, 169-178.

[102] Simons, 285-286.

[103] Suchlicki, *Columbus to Castro,* 156.

[104] Suchlicki, *Columbus to Castro,* 156.

[105] Suchlicki, *Columbus to Castro,* 183-186.

[106] Simons, 180.

[107] Andres Suarez, *Cuba: Castroism and Communism, 1959-1966* (Cambridge, Massachusetts: The Massachusetts Institute of Technology Press, 1967), 35-44.

[108] Suarez, 48.

PART III

CASTRO'S SUCCESS

In turning to the reasons for Castro's success, it is appropriate to analyze the most common theories and to dispel some popular misconceptions. First, to this day, there are those who believe that Castro ascended to power primarily due to Cuba's underdevelopment and socio-economic problems. However, in 1953, Cuba's yearly per capita income was $325 while Italy's was $307, Austria's $290, Spain's $242, Japan's $197, and the US' $1,908."[1] Cuban workers reaped approximately 67% of the gross national income compared to 59% for Argentina, 48% for Brazil and 70% for the US. according to the 1956 US Commerce Report, the Cuban people had "one of the highest standards of living in Latin America."[2] In 1958, the average wage for a Cuban agricultural worker, for an eight-hour day was $3.00 compared to $2.70 for Belgium, $1.74 for France, $2.73 for West Germany and $4.06 for the United States.[3] Savings increased from $140 million to $385.5 million between 1951 and 1957 and private construction totaling $53 million in 1952 rose to $77 million by 1957. Likewise, public construction rose form $96 million to $195 million within the same time period.[4]

Claims of widespread illiteracy and lack of medical attention were highly inflated. Free and compulsory education was established in 1901. By 1933, only about 70% of the population ten years of age and older could read. However, in the 1930s measures were

45

taken to improve elementary education in the rural areas and the number of vocational and secondary schools had dramatically increased by the mid-1950s. By then, there were three state universities with an enrollment of over 20,000. The private schools, of all levels, and the three private universities ranked near the top among Latin American schools and universities. Although there was disparity in the level of services available in the rural areas in general, Cuba's mortality rate was fifteen per 1,000 persons and it had a higher production of medical professionals than any other Caribbean nation.[5]

Clearly, sugar production, which was Cuba's primary source of national revenue beginning in the 1920s, had a direct impact on Cuba's economic, political and social systems. As would be expected, when world market demand and prices were high, as was the case during the periods of the First and Second World Wars, the Cuba economy expanded and when demand and prices were low the economy and the people suffered. For example, the price per pound of Cuban sugar rose from about two cents in 1914[6] to an all-time high of almost twenty-three cents in the first part of 1920.[7] Likewise, Cuban imports rose from \$53.73 million in 1913 to \$76.13 million in 1917.[8]

The resurgence of the European and Asian sugar beet market, Cuba's overproduction, and the world economic crisis of 1929, reduced sugar prices to an all-time low of eight cents per pound by October of 1920[9] and had a devastating impact on all aspects of the Cuban economy. Production fell from five million tons between 1924 to 1925 to two million tons between 1932 and 1933. The price per pound for sugar also fluctuated from about 1.72 cents per pound in 1929 to 0.57 cents in 1932. Additionally, the wages of field workers were cut from \$1.60 in 1929 to \$0.25 a day in 1933.[10] Salaries of urban workers were also cut by about 60%.[11]

However, the Second World War came to the rescue and sugar production rose from two and one-half million tons valued at $130 million in 1941 to four million tons with a value of $330 million in 1944.[12] The price per pound rose from approximately three cents per pound in the first years of the war to four cents in 1952 and nearly six cents during the Korean War.[13]

Beginning in 1945, the Cuban economy experienced modest, incremental growth of its industrial centers. The index of total industrial production rose from 67.24 in 1945 to 88.13 in 1951. The manufacturing sector (non-sugar) also rose from 66.21 in 1945 to 94.67 in 1945. Growth in the electricity and gas sectors was impressive rising from 48.51 in 1945 to 83.12 in 1951. Import of consumer purchases rose from 136.1 million pesos in the period of 1940-1945 to 229.1 million pesos in 1946. The decline from 436.4 pesos in 1947 to 375.7 pesos in 1949 represented a steady attempt to reduce and diversify sources of external dependence.[14]

These positive indicators do not obscure the fact that in spite of its modest progress, the Cuban economy had a long way to go toward progress and diversification. In 1956, sugar represented between 30% and 39% of the national income and between 86% and 90% of total exports.[15] In the post-Second World War period, sugar prices fell again and although the price rose to 3.5 cents per pond in 1956 during the Suez crisis, by 1959 the price of sugar was an average of 2.97 cents per pound.[16] Thus, it was highly unlikely that prices would rise to a level that would enable the country to continue to depend on sugar as its primary source of national revenue.

A second theory is that Castro's successful rise to power may be attributed to the inability of previous administrations to implement a land reform program that would "revert the land to the Cubans."[17] The perceived inequity in land distribution can actually be traced to the latter part of the nineteenth century when Spanish latifundist policy (policy of large landholdings) forced the re-concentration of landholdings and forced planters, farmers and mill owners into the cities. Re-concentration not only displaced the rural population, but also gave the United States a foothold in Cuba's economy via the purchase of tobacco, mining and sugar enterprises.[18]

However, Cuba was not "a country of mammoth landholdings with the landowners a privileged class virtually above the law."[19] In fact, "Cubans laws favored the small sugar cane farmer"[20] and while there were a number of large landholdings or latifundias, the size of the average Cuban farm had steadily declined. In 1931, the average farm was 188 acres; however, by 1946, the average size was 140 acres, compared to the 195-acre average for the US in 1945. Similarly, there had been a steady decline in the number of US landholdings in Cuba.   In 1922, seven American companies owned half of all sugar production.[21] This trend was reversed with the economic impetus provided by World War II and United States control of Cuban sugar dropped from 70% in 1928 to 35% in 1958 and Cuban ownership rose from 22% in 1939 to 62% in 1958.[22]

A third theory is that Castro's rise to power was spurred by inequity in Cuba's social system as it pertains to class structure. This theory rests on the belief that Cuba's socio-economic system consisted of a very small "upper class"[23] that consisted of plantation owners, politicians, business executives, military officers and police officials; an "intermediary"[24] class of property owners, government officials and professionals and a "working class"[25] of industrial and agricultural laborers and those who were employed in the tourist industry. According to this theory, the inability of the developing industry to absorb the growth in urban population led to the stagnation and political activism of the middle class and while the middle class was preoccupied with amassing wealth and engaged in politics as a means to rise to the high class, the high class was content to preserve the status quo.[26] One aspect of this theory is accurate; the middle and high classes were content with their economic status. However, by 1957, the high class was concerned that failure to restore political stability would impair continued economic development and tried to persuade Batista to hold new elections. Similarly, the middle class understood it had much to loose from the political chaos of the late 1950s.

Batista did not face his greatest opposition from "a Cuban proletariat that had lost ground economically as well as politically."[27] Rather, the middle class university students, writers, intellectuals and professionals took up the banner of the revolutionary movement and the 26 July Movement found its greatest support in the urban cells formed by the students, organized labor, and other urban and civic organizations.[28]

Cuba's racial makeup and the erroneous assumption that Castro was responsible to eliminating discrimination have also been offered as factors contributing to his success. Whereas there is no doubt that this aspect of the Spanish culture and nurture existed in Cuban society in 1958, race relations had never surfaced as a contentious socio-economic issue since the uprising of the Independent Color Association in 1908.[29] Undoubtedly, the Afro-Cuban and mulatto populations were disproportionally represented at the lower spectrum of Cuba's socio-economic structures. However, this was more a product of the historically short period of time since the abolition of slavery in 1886 and not due to institutionalized racism within Cuban society.

As previously discussed, Cuba's population was the most integrated of the American colonies to include the British colonies of North America.[30] The sentiment of the Afro-Cuban and mulatto populations was aptly expressed in 1872 by General Antonio Maceo, the mulatto leader of the Ten Years' War, in response to concern that he aspired to establish a Negro republic, "I must protest energetically that neither now nor at any other time am I to be regarded as an advocate of a Negro republic....this concept is a deadly thing to the democratic Republic which is founded on the basis of liberty and fraternity."[31]   This sentiment was echoed in 1908 when the Independent Color Association garnered criticism for the 1908 rebellion from distinguished black leaders to include black members of the Cuban Senate.[32]

The situation was no different in September of 1960 when Castro traveled to New York City to address the United Nations. When the Cuban delegation was asked to pay in advance for accommodations at the Shelbourne Hotel, Castro considered erecting tents in Central Park; however, he decided the Fair Play for Cuba Committee's suggestion to move to the Hotel Theresa in Harlem would constitute a much greater embarrassment for the United States. Castro's also exploited this incident to gain international recognition by forming a link between Cuba, Afro-Americans, and the third-world African continent.[33]

These residents of Harlem and the Fair Play for Cuba Committee leader who gave Castro a statue of Lincoln engraved, "From one liberator to another,"[34] did not know that racial discrimination was not a political issue for a nation whose white and black population had integrated creating a nationalistic Creole population. This is not to say that Cuban society was free of racial prejudice. However, in Cuba, there was a definite distinction to be made between personal prejudice at the personal level and institutional discrimination. Notwithstanding, a post-Castro Cuba will have to deal with the issue of racial prejudice and guard against the emergence of institutional discrimination in the process of integrating the predominantly white exile and the Afro-Cuban and mulatto island populations.

The current population of Cuba is estimated to be over 60% to 70% Afro-Cuban and mulatto.[35] "This is a sharp increase over 1959, not least because most of the emigrants were white."[36] However, in spite of "the socio-economic emancipation of blacks [which] reflects the Revolution's program to improve the lot of the lower classes, in which Afro-Cubans just 'happened' to be over-represented,[37] leading government positions and economic benefits remain are almost exclusively reserved for the white segment of the Communist population. Afro-Cubans and mulattoes have limited access to the dollar economy fueled by Cuban-American community and are "understandably frightened by the prospect of a return of the predominantly white Cubans."[38]

Meanwhile, "there seems to be something of a white backlash here and there in Cuba. Some identify the black Cubans with the failed revolution….[and] others blame Afro-Cubans for an alleged disproportional involvement with subversion and the illegal economy."[39] Regardless, racial discrimination was not a factor contributing to Castro's rise to power or to the success of the revolution. The issue of race surfaced as yet another diversionary tactic that enabled Castro to "divide and conquer" within and to export the Cuban revolutionary model throughout Latin America and the African continent under the auspices of freeing the oppressed.

The final factor proposed to have contributed to Castro's rise to power and the success of the revolution, was the State Department. In respect to the 26 July Movement, the State Department is reported to have recommended and negotiated the United States arms embargo that contributed to the demoralization of the Cuban army and crippled the Batista regime's struggle against the revolutionaries. As previously discussed, the embargo deprived the army of needed equipment and, more importantly, dealt the regime a fatal psychological blow vis-à-vis the Cuban population. In regard to Castro's rise to power, there is evidence to suggest that those who were in a position to influence US policy were either not qualified to assess the political situation or too eager to dismiss warnings that Castro was not the humanist, anti-communist, agrarian reformer. The US Ambassador to Cuba, Earl T. Smith, was among those who opposed Batista's cruelty; however, he was convinced Castro was a communist with an anti-American agenda.[40]

Ambassador Smith opposed the arms embargo and in December of 1958 and submitted a plan to Washington calling for Aguero, the President-elect, to temporarily assume the office of the president for a six-month period proceeding United Nations-supervised elections. The plan also called for the US to ship the equipment Cuba had paid for so that the army could continue to oppose Castro and his men.[41] According to Lazo, Ambassador Smith reported the State Department rejected the plan purporting there could be no solution as long as Batista remained in Cuba."[42] In other words, Batista was required to distance himself from Cuban affairs and to leave Cuba before the State Department would consider any options for a post-Batista government. In the end, Ambassador Smith seemed convinced the US was in favor of Castro's ascension to power.[43] Given the impression of the Ambassador, it is feasible to imagine the Cubans were equally pre-disposed to accept Castro as a "fait accompli".

The theories presented each have an element of relevance and a case can be made for the fact that these as well as other military and political elements contributed to the success of the 26 of July Movement. However, a narrow focus on these factors fails to recognize that which lies at the center of the issue; the Cuban people. Long dependent on an imperial or capitalist power for their public administration and economic well-being, the Cuban people failed to develop that for which they have been striving since 1868; a sovereign constitutional democracy. Spanish imperial and US capitalist tutelage were certainly contributing factors to the development of a mono-crop economic system that nurtured a sense of helplessness and dependency. However, men like Marti, Gomez, Maceo and Chibas highlighted these issues and attempted to build a nationalistic defiance for complacency.

Why then did Cubans fail to develop a constitutional democracy and to establish complimentary and prosperous socio-economic systems? The answer to this question can be found in the Cuban psyche going back to 1895 when the rebel Council of Government instructed Maximo Gomez to place Cuban troops under US command.[44] That is, a group of people engaged in the process of building an independent nation should not subjugate its armed forces to that of a foreign nation. Moreover, the Council of Government should have insisted on US recognition and pursued establishment of a coalition between Cuban and US armed forces. In failing to obtain political recognition and relinquishing command of its armed forces, the rebel government made it possible for the US and Spain to convert the Cuban War of Independence into the Spanish-American War. These actions also made it possible for the victorious US forces to deny Cuba representation in the Treaty of Paris negotiations that reduced the issue of Cuban independence to Article I in which Spain relinquished sovereignty of Cuba and the US was authorized to occupy the island for "the protection of life and property."[45]

The Treaty of Paris did not, in and of itself, deprive Cubans of their independence. From 1901 to 1958, there were political crossroads that offered Cubans an opportunity to assert their sovereignty and dedicate themselves to the task of building a democratic, prosperous nation. In 1901, the members of the Constitutional Assembly had the opportunity to resist US demands to incorporate the Platt Amendment in the Cuban Constitution.[46] The threat of alternative and indefinite US military occupation may have been easier to make than to enforce especially if the Cubans had responded with a peaceful and protracted rebellion. Instead, the Cuban leadership chose the path of least resistance believing that the US would pull out once they believed the Cubans capable of governing themselves.[47]

Beginning with the Estrada administration in 1906, Cuban presidents would look to the US for political and/or economic support. The men who rose to occupy Cuba's highest political office were a product of their Spanish culture and nurture and a Criollo political system permeated by graft and corruption. Cubans failed to unite in opposition and to create a political system in which its elected officials were held responsible to and constrained by law. Personal charisma and power enabled men of questionable character to obtain unrestrained power and rule the island as they would their homes.

In sum, the overly simplistic answer to Castro's success is that in 1959, the Cuban people were ready for a change; however, they were as unprepared or unwilling to assume responsibility for their own destiny as they had been in 1898. In 1959, when Batista fled Cuba, Cubans found their messiah. Castro was the people's choice. He transformed a nationalist movement grounded on ideals of equality and justice and designed to restore constitutional government into a personal quest for power. His rhetoric was reminiscent of the ideals first eloquently expressed by Marti and precisely what they longed to hear. Equally important, he had the support of the US. He was not elected but he was unopposed.

Notes

[1] Suarez, 34-35.

[2] US Department of Commerce, *Investment In Cuba,* (Washington D.C.: Government Printing Office, 1956); quoted in Mario Lazo, *American Foreign Policy Failures in Cuba A Dagger in the Heart* (New York: Twin Circle Publishing, 1968), 96.

[3] Lazo, 98.

[4] Lazo, 101.

[5] Lazo, 105-107.

[6] Morley, 101.

[7] Simons, 226.

[8] Morris Hyman Morley, *Toward a Theory of Imperial Politics: United States Policy and the Processes of State Formation, Disintegration and Consolidation in Cuba, 1898-1978* (Ph.D. diss., State University of New York at Binghamton, 1980), 102.

[9] Morley, 102.

[10] Morley, 137.

[11] Morley, 138.

[12] Phillip W. Bonsal, *Castro and the United States* (Pittsburg: University of Pittsburg Press, 1971), 241.

[13] Bonsal, 240-242.

[14] Morley, 226.

[15] Bonsal, 243.

[16] Bonsal, 242.

[17] Fidel Castro, *"History Will Absolve Me"; extract printed in Geoff Simons, Cuba: From Conquistador to Castro* (New York: St Martin's Press, 1996), app. 6, p. 356.

[18] Lazo, 98.

[19] Lazo, 98.

[20] Lazo, 98.

[21] Simons, 181.

[22] Lazo, 99.

[23] Morley, 246.

[24] Morley, 246.

[25] Morley, 247.

[26] Morley, 243-248

[27] Morley, 279.

[28] Suchlicki, *Columbus to Castro,* 147-152.

[29] Suchlicki, *Columbus to Castro,* 90-91.

[30] Lazo, 14.

[31] Antonio Maceo; quoted in Jaime Suchlicki, *Cuba from Columbus to Castro and Beyond,* 4th ed. (Washington: Brassey's 1997), 70.

[32] Suchlicki, *Columbus to Castro,* 90-91.

[33] Simons, *Columbus to Castro,* 288-290.

[34] Simons, 289.

[35] Gert Oostindie, *A Loss of Purpose: Crisis in Transition in Cuba,* Cuban Studies Association Occasional Paper Series, vol. 2, no. 2, March 15, 1997 (Cuban Studies Association, 1997), 18.

Notes

[36] Oostindie, *A Loss of Purpose: Crisis in Transition in Cuba,* 15.

[37] Oostindie, *A Loss of Purpose: Crisis in Transition in Cuba,* 14.

[38] Oostindie, *A Loss of Purpose: Crisis in Transition in Cuba,* 17.

[39] Oostindie, *A Loss of Purpose: Crisis in Transition in Cuba,* 17.

[40] Lazo, 159

[41] Lazo, 176.

[42] Lazo, 177.

[43] Lazo, 177.

[44] Simons, 202.

[45] *The Treaty of Peace Between the United States and Spain.*

[46] Simons, 211-212.

[47] Simons, 202.

PART IV

CASTRO'S CONTINUED SURVIVAL

Almost forty-one years later, Castro omnipotently rules over the eleven million people who did not flee or were born into the "uninterrupted revolution".[1] Those who believe his dictatorship an abomination comparable to that of Stalin, Mussolini and Hitler are perplexed by its staying power and by the fact that internal or external forces have not deposed it. Looking at its incredible staying power, there are several factors that contribute to its survival. These factors will be addressed as they relate to the previous discussion on factors proported to have contributed to the success of the revolution. Specifically, this part will analyze post-revolutionary developments in the: socio-economic system, land distribution policy, and social structure and review the impact of US policy on Cuba's socio-political development.

SOCIO-ECONOMIC FACTORS

The Economic System

In the first decade of the revolution, "the transformation of Cuba's private enterprise system into a centralized state-controlled economy resulted in growing inflation, disorganization; and bureaucratic chaos and inefficiency."[2]

Beginning in 1960, Castro implemented socio-economic reforms in line with goals outlined in the "First Havana Declaration." Having condemned "large scale landowning as a source of poverty for the peasant,"[3] "a backward and inhuman system of agricultural production,"[4] and "starvation wages,"[5] Castro proceeded to implement land reform, income redistribution and collectivization programs. He expropriated and nationalized foreign and domestic enterprises to include the utility companies, the mass communication media and the banking systems.[6]

In 1960, "Castro was sympathetic to the view's of Guevara [who was not an economist] and others who held that the wicked capitalists had inflated sugar production in Cuba so that the people of the island were slaves of a colonial plantation economy."[7] Guided by these inputs, Castro made the decision to take land out of sugar production and to implement an ambitious agricultural diversification program "hoping to lessen dependence upon sugar."[8] Under the leadership of Che Guevara, the government moved too quickly in implementing its strategy of agricultural diversification and rapid industrialization overextending the allocation of natural resources.[9] In order to ameliorate the economic situation, Castro and Guevara pursued trade and credit agreements with China and the Soviet Union.

In January of 1960, the Soviets agreed to buy 425,000 tons of sugar from Cuba in 1960 and to provide Cuba $100 million in credit for "plants, machinery and technical assistance."[10] In their second major trade agreement, Cuba agreed to provide the Soviets sugar in exchange for Soviet oil. In July of 1960, when the US oil companies in Cuba refused to process the oil, Castro nationalized them. In turn, President Eisenhower cancelled Cuba's sugar quota.[11]

In the early years of the revolution, the economic inefficiencies of the new centralized system were made worse by the economic retaliatory measures enacted by the Eisenhower and Kennedy administrations. In October of 1960, President Eisenhower imposed a partial economic embargo of Cuba prohibiting all exports with the exception of food, medicine and medical supplies. However, Castro was able to off-set these loses. In November of 1960, China and Cuba entered into a trade agreement whereby China gave Cuba $60 million of credit to purchase equipment and technical assistance and agreed to buy a million tons of sugar in 1961.[12] This was followed by another Soviet agreement to purchase nearly three million tons of sugar at four cents per pound in 1961.[13] In the same year, Cuba produced 6.7 million tons of sugar (largest harvest since the nearly eight million tons in 1952), but by 1962 the crop had dwindled to 4.8 tons.[14]

Due to the policy failures of the Central Planning Board, Cuba's new centralized economic system produced growing inflation. The high and middle classes lost their property and either migrated to the US or was absorbed into the lower class. Agricultural production declined and, in 1961, food rationing was implemented for the first time in Cuba's history.[15] On January 3, 1961, the Eisenhower administration broke diplomatic relations with Cuba and, on February 7, 1962, President Kennedy extended the partial embargo to a total embargo. The only exceptions were the non-subsidized sale of food and medicines. This embargo was further extended in March of 1962 to include all imports of goods made from Cuban materials or containing any Cuban parts.[16]

The 1963 sugar harvest was four million tons. This was the lowest in twenty years. By 1964, Castro was prepared to "end his war on sugar"[17] and "ordered a comeback of monoculture. It had taken a communist revolution to restore sugar to the place it had held in the bad old days of American domination."[18]   In reality, the Soviets persuaded Castro to adopt the socialist division of labor model under which Cuba once again concentrated on the production of sugar and nickel.   In a complete reversal of his position, Castro vowed that Cuba would produce ten tons of sugar per year.[19]   In effect, from 1964 to 1969, sugar production never achieved the 6.7-ton high of 1961, the year in which Castro was intent on eradicating the impact of sugar on the Cuban economy.[20]   By the late 1960s, "long-term trade agreements with the Soviets were perpetuating Cuba's role as a sugar producer, forcing her to abandon indefinitely any plans for significant diversification and industrialization."[21]

The early to mid 1970s were good years for the Cuban economy primarily due to a rise in the price of sugar. Cuba's Gross Domestic Product (GDP) rose from 3.9% for the years 1966 through 1970 to 12% for the years 1970 to 1974. Sugar prices also rose from 20.83 cents in 1973 to 65.39 cents in 1974.   As a result of the increased capital availability, Cuba's imports rose from 30% to 48%.   However, when sugar prices dropped to as low as eight in 1976, Cuba's combined trade (imports and exports) the non-socialist world, fell from 41.2% in 1974 to 37.0% of total trade by 1976. The decline in sugar prices drove the GDP growth rate down to seven percent in 1976 and the deficit increased from $130 million in 1974 to $560 million by the end of 1976.[22]   In the last years of the decade, diseases and other natural disasters, affected the cattle and sugar industries further hampering the economy.[23]   The economic austerity of the late 1970s coupled with the visits of over 100,000 exiles to Cuba in 1978, led to social and political unrest that resulted in the "exodus of over 125,000 Cubans in the Freedom Flotilla of

1980."[24] The exodus helped to relieve the internal pressure and to temporarily divert the focus of the island population.

In the third decade of the revolution, the "popular expectations of rapid economic improvement, [fueled by the sugar boom of the mid-1970s], were replaced by pessimism."[25] Underemployment and labor productivity reached all time lows. Worker absenteeism, theft, graft and corruption became commonplace as "Cuban's rejected socialist morality and laws and struggled to survive on a daily basis."[26] Beginning in 1980, reforms were introduced to affect some decentralization of the economy, wage reforms and bonus incentives in order to motivate workers and to increase production. The free peasant market was also introduced as a means to increase food production. In these markets, farmers were allowed to surplus goods at market demand prices after meeting government quotas. In spite of the fact that "the 1980-1985 period marked the largest gains in gross output"[27] the economy continued to deteriorate and Cuba "relied on the Soviets for massive infusions of aid to meet minimal investment and consumption needs and depended almost entirely on Soviet oil exports for energy requirements."[28] Due to the fall of sugar prices, export sales to non-communist block countries dropped from 22% in 1977 to 13% in 1982.[29]

In 1986, some of the economic reforms, to include the Peasant Free Market, were rescinded based on the fact that they were inconsistent with the goals of the revolution.[30] In particular, it was determined that the Peasant Free Market, was "creating a class of rich peasant and middle men, thereby undermining Cuba's socialist society."[31] In reality, Castro was not only concerned with the effect personal profit would have on the "socialist man," but more importantly, on its ability to alter the social structure and to potentially weaken the regime's political power. Under the auspices of returning Cuba to a "moral economy,"[32], Castro implemented an economic "Rectification Process"[33] re-centralizing and assuming personal control over all economic decisions.[34] Not surprisingly, the new centralization effort, stifled productivity and coincided with Soviet attempts to increase productivity on the part of its client states. The state-controlled economy continued to impair motivation and efficiency. Graft and corruption became a common way to circumvent government inefficiencies and to provide for common necessities.[35] Moreover, there was a continued dependence on sugar and Soviet subsidies that were just beginning to dwindle.

In the early 1990s, the collapse of Communism in the Eastern block countries followed by that of the Soviet Union devastated the Cuban economy. "Severe shortages of...petroleum, fertilizers, spare parts, raw materials, and foodstuff crippled the economy."[36] Cubans entered the "Special Period in a Time of Peace"[37] and Castro implemented an economic austerity program to meet the island's economic crisis. Under this program, food, consumer goods, gasoline and oil products were further rationed. The workweek and hours were reduced, government workers re-assigned "to more 'productive' jobs in industry and agriculture"[38] and several industrial plants were closed.[39]

In 1991, the Fourth Congress of the Communist Party "approved the regime's efforts to attract foreign investment and technology."[40] Although the law that actually established Foreign Direct Investment was passed in 1982, the Cuban government did not fully support FDI (with the exception of the hotel industry) until after the demise of the Soviet Union when it became obvious that the government could not survive without an influx of foreign capital. The regime's new economic strategy focuses FDI in Cuba's external economy and does not provide for foreign investment or joint ventures in the internal economy or the sugar industry.[41] The value of these joint ventures increased from $500 million in 1997[42] to $2.2 billion by August 1998.[43] However, they remain risky due to the island's inherent social, political and economic inefficiencies, its inability to compete with modern industrialized nations and the volatile nature of its political system.[44]

Cuba's largest source of foreign income is remittances from Cuban exiles living in the United States and Europe. In 1992, the Cuban government enacted legislation enabling Cuban citizens to possess dollars that can be used to purchase consumer goods in stores previously reserved for tourists, foreign diplomats and government officials and expanded the list of consumables exiles can send relatives in Cuba.[45] It is estimated that in 1997 alone, Cuban exiles sent approximately $600 to $800 million to relatives and friends living in Cuba.[46] In 1997, the Cuban government also increased the number of visas for travel to Cuba from the US. The objective of these policies is to obtain hard currency circulated by Cuban citizens through the economy.[47] Undoubtedly, the remittances are largely responsible for the leveling of the Cuban economy following the demise of the Soviet Union.[48]

At the same time, the continued "dollarization" of the economy has created a splinter dollar economy within the economy that, when coupled with the preferential treatment accorded foreigners in the tourist and medical industries, is creating a rift among the local Cuban population. The Cuban government is willing to accept the social consequences in order to secure its continued survival; however, the broad currency "transfusions" are not likely to produce the economic reforms that would improve Cuba's socio-economic condition. The reasons for these are many; however, the most restrictive aspects of the political-economic situation centers around the fact that the Cuban government continues to impose a command economy in which the government maintains control of the internal or agricultural and manufacturing sectors of the economy and limits foreign investment to those for which Cuba needs capital and technology to develop a new industry.

Throughout the 1990s, production and revenues in key centers of the economy continued to decline. Sugar production dropped from an estimated eight millions tons valued at almost $4,500 million in 1990 to slightly over three tons valued between $540-$600 million in 1998. Likewise, nickel production is down from over eight million tons valued at $4,000 million in 1990 to a little over three tons valued at $400 million dollars in 1999. The two brightest sectors of the economy appear to be the tourist and cigar industries. The tourist industry has witnessed a steady growth in both the number of tourists visiting the island and the associated revenues. In 1991, an estimated 400,000 people visited Cuba representing approximately $400 million in revenues. In 1998, the number of visitors increased to 1,400,000 and revenues averaged $1,800 million. Similarly, cigar production increased from $76.2 million (quantity available for export) valued at $114 million in 1990 to $16 million and $180 million in 1998.[49]

In light of these facts, it is evident that Castro's regime survives not due to but in spite of the island's economic state. Following the soviet demise in 1991, remittances from Cuban-Americans living in the US and Europe, the island's ability to produce sustainable levels of food and the resilience of its people has ensured its survival.

The Medical System

In the first year of the Castro regime, free "pre-cradle to grave"[50] health care was made available to all Cubans. Beginning in the 1970s, a significant gain was reported in the area of infant mortality that was markedly reduced from 38.7 per thousand in 1970 to 9.9 in 1994. In comparison, the second lowest rate in Latin America was that of Costa Rica at 14 per thousand and the highest was Bolivia's at 78.[51] Cuba is reported to have an enviable "vaccination programme"[52] covering 95% of its children, and "sophisticated medical products Cuba itself manufactures."[53] As of 1989, Cuba is also reported to have 263 hospitals.[54] According to Simons, "The Cuban approach to health care is impressive at all levels-from the scale of preventive medicine, through the treatment of disease by family doctor or hospital, to the highest reaches of fundamental research."[55]

On the other hand, recent reports document a decline in Cuba's medical system.

> *Few political myths in the contemporary world have proven more durable than the notion that medicine in Communist countries is somehow superior in quality and service to that offered in the West, particularly in the United States. For some inexplicable reason, the collapse of the Soviet Empire and the embarrassing revelations in its wake have done little to diminish the notion as far as it applies to one of the world's few remaining Communist states: Fidel Castro's Cuba[56].*

In effect, Cuba's medical system appears to be in deplorable condition. The people lack needed medicines, medical equipment is in a state of disrepair and training is outdated. Contrary to popular belief, these conditions are not a result of the US embargo since the embargo has never prohibited the export of medicine or medical supplies subject to proper licensing. Moreover, if the embargo were prohibitive in nature, then it would impact not only the Cuban population, but also tourists and those in the government's key leadership positions. However, there are numerous reports that attest to the fact that Cuba has developed a medical tourist industry.[57]

In a report smuggled out of Cuba in 1998, Dr. Hilda Molina, the founder of Havana's International Center for Neurological Restoration and former member of the Cuban National Assembly, reported that, although Castro had professed to oppose charging anyone, including foreigners, for medical services[58], beginning in 1989, the Cuban government, "established mechanisms designed to turn the medical system into a profit making enterprise for the government."[59] Dr. Molina also reported "enormous disparity in the quality of health services"[60] and "rewards for hospitals that give priority to foreign patients over Cuban."[61] On the quality of medical care, she stated, "The lack of adequate professional qualifications, the absence of medical ethics, and the drive to financial enrichment, also characterize Cuba's medical system."[62] Dr. Molina detailed acts of sexual abuse, theft and drug trafficking that occur as a result of indulgences or ignorance on the part of hospital administrators. Marc Falcoff, Resident Scholar in Foreign Policy at the American Enterprise Institute in Washington D.C. added, "Foreign patients are lured to Cuba with promises of non-existent treatments or cures for diseases where none exist….they are prescribed Cuban drugs they do not need, merely to increase the size of the bill."[63]

In 1998, a survey was commissioned to gather public opinion data about Cuba. The target population was Cuban immigrants who had been in the US for a period of less than three months, immigrants arriving at the Miami International Airport, and others identified via relief and Catholic charities. The survey participants appropriately varied in gender, race, educational background, occupation and income.[64] One of the interest areas on the survey was "Health Attainment"[65] Of the 1023 participants surveyed from December of 1998 to April of 1999,[66] 53% indicated the health care system improved, 90% cited free medical services as the government's greatest accomplishment and gave favorable ratings to the quality (53%) and quantity (52%) of service.[67] Eighty-nine percent indicated they would like to retain the current medical system in a post-Castro Cuba. However, in regards to the future, 98% felt a "free-market economy [would] allow for a better medial care system."[68] One explanation for this inconsistency is "that respondents assumed that under a free-market economy, medicines and medical equipment would be available"[69] to support a socialist medical system consisting of one doctor for every 200 people.[70]

Survey participants identified the following deficiencies: training of medical staff (10%), hospital availability (18%), the need to pay in dollars (39%), long surgical waiting periods (64%), insufficient technology (70%), favoritism in providing medical services to foreigners (72%), and lack of medicines (92%). Of the 98% of the participants who acknowledged tourists and Cubans are treated in separate facilities, 99% indicated the tourist facilities are better.[71]

In conclusion, the Cuban medical system appears to have significantly improved the lives of those who could not previously afford to pay for medical services. However, beginning in the late 1980s, the austere economy and the emergence of the medical tourism have led to the deterioration of the medical system. Thus, Cuba's medical system can be classified as a factor contributing to the survival of the Castro regime in the two and a half decades following the revolution. However, beginning in the late

1980s, the medical system began to suffer from chronic shortages and inefficient training that, in the long run, will negatively impact the quality of life of the Cuban people.

The Education System

In regards to education, expenditures tripled in the first three years of Castro's regime[72] and the government is reported to have wiped out the 30% illiteracy rate that existed in 1959.[73] Free and compulsory education was made available to all children and, by 1995, 100% of the children 5-year old and over were enrolled in kindergarten and above. Pre-elementary education was established, childcare centers were built and special institutions chartered to train teachers, doctors, engineers and other professionals.[74]

Those who participated in the 1998 survey of Cuban immigrants, 67% indicated education has improved under the Castro regime; however, there is a disturbing decline in university enrollments with a drop from the highest recorded enrollment of 250,000 to 100,000 in 1999. Factors contributing to the improvement of the education system are: its cost-free status (93%), availability regardless of race (72%), instructor competency (60%) and cost-free supplies (58%).[75] Overall, 90% of the survey participants support maintaining these benefits in a post-Castro Cuba.[76]

The deficiencies cited by the survey participants are that: education is politicized, "with ideology given more priority than knowledge"[77] (84%), study materials are scarce (58%), there is a "lack of freedom in choosing a career"[78] (56%), students are required to participate in a mandatory work-study programs (49%), there is a lack of employment upon graduation (46%), and there is a "requirement to join the revolution to have access to education (18%).[79] Undoubtedly, the Castro regime has increased the number of schools and educational programs. Moreover, the cost-free status and availability have made it possible for all Cubans to achieve higher levels of education. However, the more relevant issue, and one that cannot be readily analyzed, is the quality of the education. Moreover, 75% of the survey participants reported advanced education is not profitable. This is due to the fact that the government does not allow professionals to earn wages in dollars and the average person can earn more performing menial work in the tourist or dollar sector of the economy.[80]

In conclusion, in the past forty-one years, the Castro regime made great strides in making education available to all of its citizens. Although the education system has produced an unprecedented number of graduates in both technical and professional fields, it is difficult to assess the quality of that education. The most disturbing aspect of the situation is that over the last ten years, the "dollarization" of the economy "is providing upside down economic incentives to the detriment of the country's manpower quality. The impact of this regime policy on Cuba's long-term development potential is very negative."[81]

Land Distribution Policy

The issue of large "latifundias" or large landholdings had been a contentious one since the 1920s. In fact, the 1940 Constitution provided for the "limitation of the size of landholdings and the separation of the ownership of sugar mills and plantations."[82] However, the legislation had not been fully implemented because it was not necessarily in the best interest of the Cuban and American business sectors. Notwithstanding, progress had been made "particularly in giving security of tenure to tenants and even squatters in the sugar sector."[83] In the years immediately preceding the revolution, evictions of those cultivating occupied lands were practically non-existent.

In 1953, Castro claimed there were "five hundred thousand farm laborers who [lived] in miserable shacks, who [worked] four months of the year and [starved] the rest, sharing their misery with their children, who [didn't] have an inch of land to till and whose existence would move any heart not made of stone"[84] In the same speech, "History Will Absolve Me," he pledged:

> *The second revolutionary law would give non-mortgageable and nontransferable ownership of the land to all tenant and subtenant farmers, lessees, share-croppers, and squatters who hold parcels of five caballerias [165 acres] of land or less, and the state would indemnify the former owners on the basis of the rental which they would have received for these parcels over a period of ten years.[85]*

Moreover, those who, as a result of this reform, were to become new landowners would receive government assistance in obtaining equipment and training.[86] In stark contrast to his repeated pledge to "revert the land to the Cubans," [87] by the end of 1960, Castro had expropriated practically all private landholdings, Cuban and American, and placed them under government ownership.[88]

The land reforms that took place in 1959 and 1963 placed 73% of the agricultural land area under state control.[89] The Agricultural Production Cooperatives (Cooperativas de Produccion Agropecuarias) or CPAs, Cooperatives of Credit Services (Cooperativas de Credito y Servicios) or CCSs, and private farmers shared the remainder of the agricultural land area.[90]

By 1989, the state claimed 74.3% of the agricultural land area compared to 11.4% for the CPAs, 10.9% for the CCSs, and 3.4% for the private farms.[91] Historically, as would be expected, the CPAs obtained higher levels of land utilization than the state-owned farms and the CCSs. The obvious explanation being that CPAs are a cooperative of private landholders who have an incentive to cultivate higher yields because they are able to sell surpluses in the state's agricultural markets or the more profitable black market.

By 1993, "CPAs, CCSs and private farms, "utilized their land more intensively [that is, cultivated higher proportions of their agricultural land areas] than the state farms."[92] The demonstrated efficiency of these less-restrictive sectors, no doubt resulted in the creation of the Basic Units of Cooperative Production (Unidades Basicas de Produccion Cooperativa) or UBPCs in 1993. The UBPCs were established as state-owned, but less restrictive versions of the state farm. By 1996, the UBPCs accounted for 42% of Cuba's agricultural land area cultivating 64.5% of their available land.[93]

In comparison, the private farms accounted for 4.1% of the agricultural land areas of which 68.3 was cultivated.[94] In different terms, state farms had 13.8% of their land idle which was twice that of the UBPCs and private farms and more than three times higher than the CPAs and CCSs. The production capabilities of cooperative sectors (CPAs and CCSs) were also impressive. In 1997, they produced 79% of the island's vegetables, 69% of its fruits, 41% of its coffee and 84% of the tobacco.[95] The UBPCs produced more than 70% of Cuba's sugar; however, "even the Cuban government reports unprofitability of a large proportion of the UBPCs."[96]

In the same year, a number of independent farmers joined in creating a new association named the National Alliance of Independent Farmers of Cuba (Alianza Nacional de Agricultores Independientes de Cuba) or ANAIC. The founders of the first two alliances were primarily farmers who had participated in the reformist movement of the 1950s and supported the 1959 revolution. Their disillusionment with the land reform policies and the subsequent deterioration of the agrarian economy[97] led these farmers to "pursue a new and more independent avenue to solve their families' basic needs."[98] As of April of this year, there are eight ANAICs. They face obstacles from the authorities and are monitored to ensure their plans are in concert with the objectives of the revolution. However, in 1998, "they obtained a surplus that allowed them to sell their products directly to the consumers."[99] They are limited by their lack of equipment and supplies, but if they remain profitable in the face of continued scarcity on a national level, they may be able to obtain the needed internal and external support.

In closing, an interesting aspect of the land distribution and food production, distribution and consumption patterns is that, while fool supplies in the state ration stores are not sufficient to meet the needs of the population, the agricultural markets are providing approximately "60% of the daily caloric consumption"[100] albeit at a higher cost to the Cuban people. The significant aspect of this is that the private sectors produce enough to sell in the agricultural markets after providing for the subsistence of their families, meeting the government quota (80%) and paying the associated agricultural market taxes and tariffs.[101]   These figures do not take into account the agricultural surplus that the private sector may be contributing to the black market where profit is higher since the farmer is not required to pay taxes or tariffs.

These facts indicate that the regime has done little to rectify the land distribution deficiencies Castro himself identified in 1953. In fact, the regime's policies displaced farmers causing a mass exodus to the cities in the early years of the revolution.[102] Also, by using agrarian labor as a punishment tool for those who committed infractions in their

73

workplace and those who were on a waiting list to migrate from Cuba, the government de-moralized the farmer and marginalized the agrarian sector of the economy. Finally, the collectivization process led to apathy on the part of the farmer who was required to work long, hard hours and was unable to keep enough food to provide for the daily subsistence of his family.[103]

Thus, if there is credit to be assessed within the agricultural sector for the success and sustainment of the Castro regime, it must be given to the private sectors (CPAs and CCSs and private farms) of the agrarian community that are, in effect, keeping the Cuban people from starving.

Social Structure

In a socio-cultural context, the revolutionary ideals condemning "the discrimination against the Negro….[and] the inequality and exploitation of women,"[104] led to an increase in the number of Afro-Cubans in schools, universities and white-collar positions.[105] At the same time, government leadership positions remain almost exclusively filled by white males. Since 1953, there has been a deliberate attempt to garner the support of the Afro-Cuban population. Some believe this is a realistic political approach in light of the fact that Afro-Cubans are an estimated 60% to 70% of the Cuban population. Others assert the strategy gives Castro international appeal and greater control of the Afro-Cuban population. In a similar fashion, the government's acceptance of Afro-Cuban religions to include Santeria and Palo Monte, give the government a façade of religious tolerance and accommodation, a profitable enterprise for the tourist industry and increased Afro-Cuban support of the regime.[106]

Meanwhile, Afro-Cubans are still disproportionately represented in the "lower" class and their chances of rising to the "middle" or "high" class in Cuba's dollar economy are limited since the exile community that which feeds this economy is predominantly white and the remittances flow from white Cuban-Americans to their white relatives and friends. Therefore, the Afro-Cubans' share of this economic sector will likely be limited by the extent to which they can access the tourist or dollar economy. Consequently, although "the Afro-Cuban population has made the most relative progress since 1959, this advance is quickly being annihilated by the present [economic] crisis."[107] Currently, Afro-Cuban youths are prominently represented in all sectors of the illegal economy to include prostitution. Conversely, to the dismay of the regime, Afro-Cubans are also well represented in dissident organizations.[108]

The Castro regime has also created "a new and more militant role for women."[109] Women now fill positions previously unavailable to them and more women are university graduates than before; however, women are also underrepresented in government positions.[110] Unfortunately, the rise of the tourist industry also created a new opportunity for the Cuban woman as a "jinetera" (prostitute) benefiting from "sex tourism"[111] and Cuba has gone full circle back to 1959 when Havana was described "as the brothel of the US."[112] Cuban women are increasingly shouldering the responsibility for the financial support of their families as well as the housekeeping and childcare. Many of the men who leave Cuba report leaving families behind. Likewise, the "jineteras" report they have to care for a child or children without the support of a father.[113]

In the process of creating the socialist state, the Castro regime may have irrevocably altered the Cuban family. Many children attend state schools away from home and see their parents at select times during the year. [114] Recently, a father was sentenced to seven months in jail for not allowing his fourth grade son to join the Young Pioneers group at school. The boy's principal and teachers accused the father of "actions contrary to the normal development of a minor."[115] The governing directive, Law 87, Section II, Article 135 (1), also makes it a crime punishable with up to one year in jail for anyone, parents included to encourage a minor to leave home, to miss school, to refuse educational work inherent in the national system [to refuse to attend work camps] or to disregard his/her obligations as they relate to the respect and love of the Nation."[116] In this manner, the Cuban government makes it a crime for parents to raise their children in accordance with their personal values and prohibits them from imparting their personal social, religious and political beliefs.

If the future of any society rests with the education and upbringing of its youth, the future of Cuban society is in jeopardy. Currently Cuban youths view advanced education as a waste since it leads to jobs in the less lucrative state-controlled sectors of the economy. Additionally, civil disobedience and criminal activity are increasingly tolerated and accepted as they are quick and sure solutions to economic necessity.[117] There are also indications that teen pregnancy; early marriage and divorce are on the rise.[118] The government has actively encouraged the demoralization of society, "perhaps aware that the only way to develop Cuba's new socialist man is through the destruction of the culture-transmitting institutions, such as the family and the church." [119] In Cuba, economic rewards and political advancement are tied to the loyalty and sacrifice demonstrated for the revolutionary cause. Therefore, men and women are subject to social pressure, coercion and or state direction to perform "voluntary" work in the cane and coffee fields.[120]

The system of "collective vigilance" established by the government in 1960[121] was the first official act toward the destruction of social institutions that threatened to development of the "socialist man."[122] This system established a Committee for the Defense of the Revolution in every street of every neighborhood throughout Cuba. The members of the committees are neighbors and their purpose is to spy on their fellow neighbors and to report to the authorities any sign of "discontent."[123] These committees do not only report on malcontents, they also take active measures to correct their behavior such as verbal and physical abuse. Thus, neighbors who had previously functioned as extended families became potential informants and repressive agents of the government.

US POLICY

Background

The final theory focuses on the role US policy may have played in the sustainment of the Castro regime. That is, did US policy give Castro the external enemy he needed to divert attention form the failures of the revolution and unify Cubans in opposition to a "Yankee Invasion"?[124] Also, did US policy drive Castro into the Marxist-Leninist camp that would keep his regime afloat for 30 years? Did US policy support the sustainment of the Castro regime?

In 1959, Castro was a devout Cuban nationalist and anti-American predisposed to break all ties between Cuba and the US. As early as 1958, in a letter to Celia Sanchez,

Castro wrote, "When this war is over, a much longer and more important war will begin for me, the war I shall wage against the Americans. I feel this is my destiny."[125]

Clearly, Castro had no intention of establishing a constitutional democracy in Cuba. If he did, he would have called for elections following Batista's departure and he would most certainly have been elected president. However, by so doing, he would have agreed to accept a limit on his power and to allow others to participate in the electoral, legislative and decision-making processes. His goal was a complete restructuring of Cuba's social, political and economic systems and to that end, he needed to divert the Cuban's attention from the political agenda (government reform) and to justify a complete control of Cuban affairs by creating an external threat and fabricating an agenda of social reform.[126]

Soon after the US recognized Cuba's revolutionary government in January of 1959, Che Guevara began to incite "the people to fight against the US Marines and to extend subversion to Latin America."[127] On February 19, 1959, when the new Ambassador, Phillip Bonsal, arrived in Cuba, Castro delivered a televised anti-American speech that Bonsal characterized as, "a thesis that feeds the Cuban ego while it wounds the American pride and self-esteem."[128] Nevertheless, Bonsal "endeavored through as many channels as possible to convey good will and readiness to enter into serious negotiation on any matters the retime might wish to raise."[129] The matters Bonsal was prepared to discuss, with the approval of the State Department, included a new tariff structure to stimulate industrialization and diversification, a proposal for a selective nationalization of US property, short-term financial assistance and Cuban participation in the operation of the

Guantanamo base. Castro did not meet with Bonsal until March at which time Castro refused to conduct any serious business.[130]

In light of these events, it is appropriate to conclude that, in 1959, the policy of the US was decidedly non-confrontational. The goal was not to alienate the Cuban regime or to make the US and enemy of the regime, but rather to develop, "a relationship of cordial confidence and to instill in [the Cuban government] a belief that the government of the United States was prepared to give the most sympathetic and constructive consideration to any proposals of the new Cuban government."[131] The fact that the US emerged as the enemy is a product of historical resentments fueled by Castro's predilections which were radically nationalistic and anti-American.[132] In 1960, there was, as will be discussed later, a dramatic change in US policy; however, in the early part of 1959, US policy was unquestionably pro-Castro.[133]

In this context, what accounts for Castro's decision to form an alliance with the Soviet Union? A discussion of whether or no he was a Marxist-Leninist prior to his proclamation of fact in December of 1961 is irrelevant. The relevant factor is Castro's political goals vis-à-vis Cuba's political climate. Throughout 1959, Castro was preoccupied with creating the political agenda lacking in his 26 July Movement.[134] The "seed" of the creation was not communism; it was Castro himself. In fact, there are several highly qualified observers who refrain from classifying Cuba as a communist nation primarily because according to communist doctrine, "the construction of socialism [presupposes] the 'leading role of the proletariat' and of its vanguard, the Communist Party."[135] The working class did, not lead the Cuban Revolution of 1959, and, when in

79

December of 1961, Castro declared the Revolution was socialist and declared himself a Marxist-Leninist, there were only three Communists serving in his regime.[136]

Thus, Castro's unique system of government has been described as "Castroism" defined as "a form of personal power, based essentially on the charismatic qualities of the leader and made possible by the complete collapse of the old state authority."[137]

Castro's goal was not to create a worker's paradise but to liberate Cuba from the imperialistic forces, to break all ties with a corrupt capitalist system, and to become the liberator of Latin America by exporting the tenets of the Cuban revolution.[138] His rapprochement to the Soviet Union was the only way to achieve these goals in a bi-polar world because, by mid-1959, the early glow of the revolution was fading. On the home front, the regime had failed to organize its administrative and defense functions. The economy was in chaos and the Cuban landowners and businessmen who were not migrating to the US were increasingly leery of Castro's reforms. Those who belonged to political parties that had been marginalized by the Batista regime were hoping for the return of normal elections. Castro knew that in order to retain personal power, he had to squelch these concerns and desires.[139] In order to do this, he adopted Che Guevara's socialist agenda for radical social reform transforming a movement designed to restore a constitutional democracy into a social "uninterrupted revolution" [140] destined to collide with the US.

Therefore, Castro had to find an ally with the political clout and economic resources to secure his position. The Soviet Union and China were potential candidates; however, in its infancy, the Castro regime was not adequately defined or readily welcomed. Thus, Castro's move toward and alliance with the Soviet Union was a deliberate and slow process in which Castro not only had to resolve internal issues involving the Cuban Communist Party, but also to navigate the currents of Sino-Soviet relations.

In 1959, the majority of the Cuban population was anti-communist; therefore, Castro found it prudent to minimally criticize and to distance himself from the party.[141] However, he did not entirely alienate them perhaps because they were one of the few groups that had some degree of organization and members of a larger hierarchical political structure. The Communist Party garnered Castro's appreciation in June of 1959 when it actively supported his unsuccessful attempt to help liberate the people of the Dominican Republic from President Trujillo's dictatorship.[142] The 225 rebels Castro sent to support the Juan Bosch opposition were killed or captured by Trujillo's troops[143] and the Communist Party was the only benefactor of the fiasco as President Urrutia was replaced President Dorticos (Communist).[144] Castro's defeat in the Dominican Republic had been shattering and led him to reverse his earlier position and to plan for the purchase of military equipment. He knew that in order to export his revolution, he needed military equipment and an ally who not only shared his anti-American predilection, but who would also be able to defend Cuba at the time of its inevitable collision with the US. By then, the US was opposed to selling weapons to Cuba and persuading other countries to refuse to do so as well.[145]

Additionally, Castro needed to find new export markets for Cuban sugar. Toward the end of 1959, the Soviet Union was the logical choice of trading partner and military ally. In 1960, US policy contributed to Cuba's economic crisis by restricting (January 1960) and eliminating (July 1960) Cuba's sugar quota. However, contrary to popular belief, Castro did no seek a Soviet alliance to improve the island's economy. Castro sought Soviet aid to obtain the military equipment he needed to stay the fabricated "OAS [Organization Of American States] conspiracy"[146] and "Yankee aggression."[147] In turn, the Soviet Union did not have altruistic motives for aiding Cuba. Soviet-American relations had deteriorated following the shooting of the U-2 over Soviet territory and there is some indication that Premier Khrushchev may have, at that point, decided to bring "further pressure on the United States, by way of Cuba."[148]

Thus, in May of 1960, the Soviets had begun to ship oil to Cuba making Cuba independent of British and American oil supplies. This arrangement made it possible for Castro to nationalize the US refineries when they refused to process the Soviet oil. In June, Cuba received its first armaments from Czechoslovakia and in July, three days after President Eisenhower cancelled the Cuban sugar quota in retaliation for the confiscation of the oil refineries, a Cuban newspaper reported that, if necessary, Khrushchev was willing to defend the Cuban people with rockets.[149]

For a time, Castro adeptly played the major communist powers against each other. In October, after the Eisenhower administration eliminated Cuba's sugar quota and established the partial embargo of Cuba, Castro sent Guevara to both the Soviet Union and China to negotiate higher sugar export agreements. Guevara was not able to reach an agreement with the Soviet Union; however, China agreed to buy a million tons of sugar in 1961 and granted Cuba a $60 million dollar credit for equipment [150] Chinese support gave Castro leverage with the Soviet Union and in December of 1960, the Soviets agreed to purchase 2,700,000 tons of sugar. However, Castro's alliance was short-lived, as China did not have the resources to help Cuba with its economic problems or to assist it in its crusade to export the Cuban revolution throughout Latin America.

By 1966, the Sino-Soviet rift caused by the Soviet's support of Vietnam placed Cuba in a difficult position and Chinese-Cuban relations soured due to differences in their ideological approaches.[151] Clearly, Castro's economic problems and political ideologies gave him no choice; he placed himself firmly in the Soviet camp where he remained until the early 1990s.

US policy did not give Castro the external enemy he needed to divert attention form the failures of the revolution and unify Cubans in opposition to a "Yankee Invasion. Castro was and remains devoutly anti-American and used "Cuba Si, Yankee No" as a diversion to consolidate and maintain absolute power. Likewise, US policy did not drive Castro into the Marxist-Leninist camp that would keep his regime afloat for 30 years. Castro needed a like-minded ally to help preserve his political dominion and to enable him to confront the US. The Soviet Union was the only like-minded nation with the requisite financial resources.

Notes

[1] Suarez, 62.

[2] Suchlicki, *Columbus to Castro,* 159.

[3] Fidel Castro, *"First Havana Declaration";* extract quoted in Geoff Simons, *Cuba from Conquistador to Castro* (New York: St Martin's Press, 1996), 363-364.

[4] Fidel Castro, *"First Havana Declaration";* extract quoted in Geoff Simons, *Cuba from Conquistador to Castro* (New York: St Martin's Press, 1996), 363-364.

[5] Fidel Castro, *"First Havana Declaration";*extract quoted in Geoff Simons, *Cuba from Conquistador to Castro* (New York: St Martin's Press, 1996), 363-364.

[6] Suchlicki, 157-158.

[7] Bonsal, 208.

[8] Suchlicki, *Columbus to Castro,* 157.

[9] Suchlicki, *Columbus to Castro,* 159.

[10] Suarez, 84.

[11] Suarez, 62.

[12] Suarez, 116-118.

[13] Suarez, 62.

[14] Lazo, 404

[15] Suchlicki, *Columbus to Castro,* 159.

[16] *Cuba,* 40-42.

[17] Lazo, 404.

[18] Lazo, 404.

[19] Lazo, 404

[20] Bonsal, 209.

[21] Suchlicki, *Columbus to Castro,* 172.

[22] Morel, 849-850.

[23] Suchlicki, *Columbus to Castro,* 204.

[24] Edward Gonzalez, *A Strategy for Dealing with Cuba in the 1980s* (Santa Monica: RAND Corporation, 1982), 28.

[25] Suchlicki, *Columbus to Castro,* 204.

[26] Suchlicki, *Columbus to Castro,* 204.

[27] Jaime Suchlicki, *Cuba: A Current Assessment,* Institute for Cuban and Cuban American Studies Occassional Paper Series, vol. 2, no. 4, May 15, 1997 (Cuban Studies Association, 1997), 3.

[28] Suchlicki, *Columbus to Castro,*204.

[29] Edward Gonzalez and David Ronfeldt, *Castro, Cuba, and the World* (Santa Monica: RAND Corporation, 1986), 81.

[30] Gonzalez and Ronfeldt, *Castro Cuba and the World,* 86.

[31] Gonzalez and Ronfeldt, *Castro Cuba and the World,* 86.

[32] Edward Gonzalez and David Ronfeldt, *Cuba Adrift in a Postcommunist World* (Santa Monica: RAND Corporation, 1992), 2.

[33] Gonzalez and Ronfeldt, *Cuba Adrift in a Postcommunist World,* 2.

[34] Gonzalez and Ronfeldt, *Cuba Adrift in a Postcommunist World,* 2.

[35] Suchlicki, *Columbus to Castro,* 204.

Notes

[36] Suchlicki, *Columbus to Castro,* 223.

[37] Gonzalez and Ronfeldt, *Cuba Adrift in a Postcommunist World,* 4

[38] Gonzalez and Ronfeldt, *Cuba Adrift in a Postcommunist World,* 4

[39] Gonzalez and Ronfeldt, *Cuba Adrift in a Postcommunist World,* 4.

[40] Gonzalez and Ronfeldt, *Cuba Adrift in a Postcommunist World,* 6.

[41] Gonzalez and Ronfeldt, *Cuba Adrift in a Postcommunist World,* 23.

[42] Jaime Suchlicki, *Cuba: A Current Assessment,* 5.

[43] Larry Press, *Cuban Telecommunications, Computer Networking, and U.S.Policy Implications* (RAND: Santa Monica, California, 1996), 41.

[44] Jaime Suchlicki, *Cuba: A Current Assessment,* 5-6.

[45] Jaime Suchlicki, *Cuba: A Current Assessment,* 4.

[46] Antonio Jorge, *The U.S. Embargo and the Failure of the Cuban Economy,* Institute for Cuban and Cuban American Studies Occassional Paper Series, February 2000, (Cuban Studies Association, 2000), 13.

[47] Jaime Suchlicki, *Cuba: A Current Assessment,* 4.

[48] Jorge, *The U.S. Embargo and the Failure of the Cuban Economy,* 13.

[49] Gary H. Maybarduk, "The State of the Cuban Economy 1998-1999" in *Association for the Study of the Cuban Economy (ASCE): Papers and Proceedings of the Ninth Annual Meeting of the Association for the Study of the Cuban Economy (ASCE),"* in Coral Gables, Florida, August 12-14, 1999, vol.9 (Silver Spring: Association for the Study of the Cuban Economy (ASCE), 1999), 1-11.

[50] Simons, 324.

[51] Simons, 28.

[52] Simons, 29.

[53] Simons, 29.

[54] Simons, 30.

[55] Simons, 30.

[56] Marc Falcoff, "Cuban Medicine and Foreign Patients", *Cuba Brief,* Summer 1998, 3.

[57]Ernesto Betancourt and Guillermo Grenier, "Measuring Cuban Public Opinon: Economic, Social, and Political Issues" in *Association for the Study of the Cuban Economy (ASCE): Papers and Proceedings of the Ninth Annual Meeting of the Association for the Study of the Cuban Economy (ASCE)",* in Coral Gables, Florida, August 12-14, 1999, vol.9 (Silver Spring: Association for the Study of the Cuban Economy (ASCE), 1999), 255.

[58] Dr. Hilda Molina, "A Cuban Doctor Reports: Cuban Medicine Today," *Cuba Brief,* Summer 1998, 3.

[59] Molina, "A Cuban Doctor Reports," 1.

[60] Molina, "A Cuban Doctor Reports," 1.

[61] Molina, "A Cuban Doctor Reports," 6.

[62] Molina, "A Cuban Doctor Reports," 5.

[63] Falcoff, " Foreign Patients," 4.

[64] Churchill Roberts, "Measuring Cuban Public Opinion: Methodology" in *Association for the Study of the Cuban Economy (ASCE): Papers and Proceedings of the*

Notes

Ninth Annual Meeting of the Association for the Study of the Cuban Economy (ASCE) in Coral Gables, Florida, August 12-14, 1999, vol.9 (Silver Spring: Association for the Study of the Cuban Economy (ASCE), 1999), 245.

[65] Betancourt and Grenier, "Cuban Public Opinon," 253-255.

[66] Roberts, "Cuban Public Opinion," 245.

[67] Betancourt and Grenier, "Cuban Public Opinon," 254.

[68] Betancourt and Grenier, "Cuban Public Opinon," 255.

[69] Betancourt and Grenier, "Cuban Public Opinon," 255.

[70] Betancourt and Grenier, "Cuban Public Opinon," 255.

[71] Betancourt and Grenier, "Cuban Public Opinon," 254.

[72] Simons, 325.

[73] Suchlicki, *Columbus to Castro,* 157.

[74] Simons, 25-26.

[75] Betancourt and Grenier, "Cuban Public Opinon," 253.

[76] Betancourt and Grenier, "Cuban Public Opinon," 253.

[77] Betancourt and Grenier, "Cuban Public Opinon," 253.

[78] Betancourt and Grenier, "Cuban Public Opinon," 253.

[79] Betancourt and Grenier, "Cuban Public Opinon," 253.

[80] Betancourt and Grenier, "Cuban Public Opinon," 253.

[81] Betancourt and Grenier, "Cuban Public Opinon," 253.

[82] Bonsal, 70.

[83] Bonsal, 70.

[84] Fidel Castro, "History Will Absolve Me"; extract printed in Geoff Simons, *Cuba: From Conquistador to Castro* (New York: St Martin's Press, 1996), 356.

[85] Fidel Castro, "History Will Absolve Me"; extract printed in Geoff Simons, *Cuba: From Conquistador to Castro* (New York: St Martin's Press, 1996), 356.

[86] Bonsal, 70.

[87] Fidel Castro, "History Will Absolve Me"; extract printed in Geoff Simons, *Cuba: From Conquistador to Castro* (New York: St Martin's Press, 1996), 356.

[88] Bonsal, 71.

[89] Antonio Alonso Perez, "Ponencia al Encuentro de Cooperativas Independienties: Medio Ambiente, Ecologia, y Su Impacto al Campesino Cubano, *CubaNet,* [article on-line accessed 4 May 2000], available from http://www.cubanet.org/cooperativa/articulo. Html; Internet.

[90] William A. Messina Jr., "Agricultural Reform in Cuba: Implications for Agricultural Production, Markets and Trade", in *Association for the Study of the Cuban Economy (ASCE): Papers and Proceedings of the Ninth Annual Meeting of the Association for the Study of the Cuban Economy (ASCE),* in Coral Gables, Florida, August 12-14, 1999, vol.9 (Silver Spring: Association for the Study of the Cuban Economy (ASCE), 1999), 434.

[91] Messina, "Agricultural Reform in Cuba," 434.

[92] Messina, "Agricultural Reform in Cuba," 435.

[93] Messina, "Agricultural Reform in Cuba," 435.

[94] Messina, "Agricultural Reform in Cuba," 435.

Notes

[95] Manuel David Orrio, "Los Guajiros Tambien Gritan Libertad!" *CubaNet* [article on-line accessed on May 4, 2000], available from http://www.cubanet.org/cooperativa/articulo.html; Internet.

[96] Messina, "Agricultural Reform in Cuba," 441.

[97] Jose Alvarez, "Independent Agricultural Cooperatives in Cuba?" in *Association for the Study of the Cuban Economy (ASCE): Papers and Proceedings of the Ninth Annual Meeting of the Association for the Study of the Cuban Economy (ASCE)* in Coral Gables, Florida, August 12-14, 1999, vol. 9 (Silver Spring: Association for the Study of the Cuban Economy (ASCE), 1999), 157.

[98] Alvarez, "Independent Agricultural Cooperatives," 157.

[99] Alvarez, "Independent Agricultural Cooperatives,"162.

[100] Messina, "Agricultural Reform in Cuba," 438.

[101] Reynaldo Hernandez Perez, "Ponencia al Encuentro de Cooperativas Independientes: Politica de Precios y Compra de los Productos Agricolas por Parte del Estado al Sector Campesino", *CubaNet ,*[on-line accessed on May 4. 2000] available from http://www.cubanet.org/cooperativa/articulo.html; Internet.

[102] Alvarez, "Independent Agricultural Cooperatives," 157.

[103] Perez, "Ponencia al Encuentro de Cooperativas Independientes."

[104] Fidel Castro, "History Will Absolve Me"; extract quoted in Geoff Simons, Cuba from Conquistador to Castro (New York: St Martin's Press, 1996), 363-364.

[105] Oostindie, 14.

[106] Oostindie, 15.

[107] Oostindie, 17.

[108] Oostindie, 17.

[109] Suchlicki, *Columbus to Castro*, 158.

[110] Suchlicki, *Columbus to Castro*, 158-159.

[111] Oostindie, 12.

[112] Oostindie, 12.

[113] Oostindie, 13-14.

[114] Suchlicki, *Columbus to Castro,*159.

[115] "From Cuba: Father Jailed For Refusing Indoctrination For His Son," [on-line accessed on May 4, 2000], *CubaNet News*, April 4, 2000; Internet available from http://www.cubanet.org/.

[116] "Modificaciones al Codigo Penal de la Republica de Cuba," [article on-line accessed on April 4, 2000], *CubaNet News*, March 3, 1999; available at http://www.cubanet.org/.

[117] Oostindie, 10.

[118] Oostindie, 13.

[119] Suchlicki, *Columbus to Castro*, 159.

[120] Suchlicki, *Columbus to Castro,* 158-159.

[121] Suarez, 108.

[122] Suchlicki, *Columbus to Castro,* 159.

[123] Suarez, 108.

[124] Suarez, 119.

Notes

[125] Roger W. Fontaine, *On Negotiating with Cuba* (American Enterprise Institute for Public Policy Research Washington D.C., 1975), 34.

[126] Suarez, 64-81.

[127] Suarez, 43.

[128] Bonsal, 38.

[129] Bonsal, 51.

[130] Bonsal, 51.

[131] Bonsal, 51.

[132] Gonzalez, Ronfelldt, *Castro, Cuba, and the World,* 13-28.

[133] Bonsal, 28-32.

[134] Suarez, 78-99.

[135] Suarez, 127.

[136] Suarez, 128.

[137] Suarez, 78.

[138] Gonzalez and Ronfelldt, *Castro, Cuba, and the World,* 13-28.

[139] Suarez, 93-98.

[140] Suarez, 63.

[141] Suarez, 79.

[142] Suarez, 69.

[143] Lazo, 195.

[144] Suarez, 69.

[145] Suarez, 70-72.

[146] Suarez, 71.

[147] Suarez, 92.

[148] Suarez, 91

[149] Suarez, 94.

[150] Suarez, 116.

[151] Suarez, 235 –236.

PART V

PAST CUBA POLICY

EISENHOWER ADMINISTRATION

The previous section covered factors purported to have contributed to Castro's success and, in particular, dismissed the fallacy that the US drove Castro into the Marxist-Leninist camp that kept his regime afloat for thirty years. However, can it be said that US policy has sustained the Castro regime? What events account for the transition from the pursuit of the demise of the Castro regime in 1960 to the promotion of "a peaceful transition to democracy in 2000? A cursory review of the Kennedy, Nixon, Johnson, Ford, Carter, Reagan, Bush and Clinton administrations will help to answer these questions.

US policy, from 1952 to 1958, was unquestionably pro-Batista and, during this period, under the auspices of "hemispheric defense,"[1] the Batista regime received over $16 million in military equipment. Toward the end of the decade, the political chaos in Cuba led to a change in US policy spearheaded by the State Department. By the end of 1958, the Department of State and the Department of Defense were at odds on the continued viability of the Batista government. On the one hand, there was a need to protect American business interests that, in the opinion of some, meant keeping Batista in power. On the other hand, there was a desire to curb the regime's growing repression and to restore social justice. In this context, the military assistance program became a critical issue. In the end, the State Department recommendation prevailed and the US imposed the arms embargo. This action marked the point at which US policy changed to support Castro in the overthrow of the Batista regime.[2]

However, the Eisenhower administration did not formally shift its position until March of 1960 when President Eisenhower realized that Che Guevara had close ties with Latin American leftist governments and that Castro had forged political and economic alliances with China and the Soviet Union.[3] At this juncture, President Eisenhower tasked the Central Intelligence Agency (CIA) to develop a plan to affect a change of government in Cuba. The plan entitled, *A Program of Covert Action Against the Castro Regime,* called for the creation of a government in exile, a propaganda campaign, an organization to perform intelligence and covert actions, and a paramilitary force for future actions.[4] Between March and November of 1960, Cuba had nationalized all US property on the island and the US had established a partial embargo. During the final months of the Eisenhower administration, the CIA developed a plan for an invasion of Cuba to form resistance cells that would, with CIA support, ultimately form a viable political and military challenge to Castro's regime.

THE KENNEDY ADMINISTRATION

The Kennedy administration's Cuba policy was based on the assessment that Castro had abandoned control of the revolution to the Soviet Union and forged an alliance that established a dichotomy of ideologies on the Western hemisphere. Prior to his inauguration Senator Kennedy stated, "Our [US] policies of neglect and indifference have let it [Cuba] slip behind the iron curtain."[5] Although he felt it was too late to save

Cuba, he declared the US would "firmly resist further communist encroachment....through a strengthened Organization of American States and encouraging those liberty loving Cubans who are leading the resistance to Castro."[6] To this end, the Kennedy administration revived earlier plans for an exile invasion of Cuba with the caveat that US sponsorship be concealed to avoid international and domestic criticism.[7]

By April of 1961, Castro's internal support appeared to be waning. Although he still had considerable popular support, there was a significant increase of counter-revolutionary activity. Once again, the university students took the lead protesting the regime's dictatorial actions. In spite of the fact that the agrarian reforms had much popular support, there was concern about the unilateral character of these actions. In addition to the students, the opposition consisted of former Castro allies, Batista supporters and the Catholic Church who became disillusioned with the direction the revolution was taking.[8]

Thus, the timing seemed right for an exile invasion. The internal opposition forces envisioned they would support the exiles through acts of sabotage to deter Castro's forces.[9] On April 17, 1961, 1,200 Cuban exiles landed in Cuba. There were several reasons for the failure of the invasion. First, the plans originally prepared by the Eisenhower administration called for the invasion forces to land in the city of Trinidad that was further from Havana and Castro's forces. Its location in the foothills of the Escambray Mountains offered an excellent fall back position and the majority of its population was believed to be anti-Castro. However, President Kennedy's advisors, primarily those from the State Department, believed Trinidad was too large and too close to the coast for the US to be able to maintain plausible deniability. Playa Giron was, in many ways, an acceptable alternative; however, it was surrounded by swamps, was sparsely populated, and did not provide an adequate fall back position.[10]

In this manner, the success of the invasion came to rest on air strikes by the Free Cuban Air Squadron trained and based in Nicaragua. Herein lies the second reason for the failure of the invasion. The air portion of the campaign originally called for two strikes of sixteen aircraft to neutralize Castro's air force consisting of thirty planes and a third strike to support the exile landings at Playa Giron and to secure the airfield. The Free Cuban Air Squadron had twenty-five aircraft. The aircraft were sixteen B-26 bombers that had been stripped of tail guns in order to carry fuel for their trip from Nicaragua to Cuba and back and nine C-54 and C-46 transport aircraft carrying troops and supplies.[11]

The land invasion forces totaled 1, 443 men whose mission was to clear the airport runway while the freighters unloaded men and supplies. By order of President Kennedy, the plan for the landing was altered and scheduled to take place under the cover of night. The air campaign was also changed; the first air strike was reduced to eight sorties and the second and third air strikes were cancelled. The initial phase of the land assault was highly successful. The troops took control of the Giron airport and were joined by over 500 local citizens and members of the local militia.[12] The first air strike failed to destroy all of Castro's Air Force and without benefit of the second or third strike forces, the men unloading the freighters and those on land were defenseless. Two freighters, one carrying weapons and munitions, were destroyed and the remaining three freighters carrying equipment were forced to leave the areas. The Free Cuban Air Squadron lost half its bombers on the first day. They continued to fly 17-hour sorties between Nicaragua and Playa Giron in order to stall Castro's advancing army; however, by April 19, the land invasion force had run out of ammunition and food and was forced to give up the fight.[13]

Although the circumstances mentioned resulted in the failure of the invasion, the root cause lies in the conflict that existed between US national interests, US policy makers, and their perception of the international political environment. In 1961, it was determined that, for political and economic reasons, Castro's overthrow was in the US national interest. However, due to the opposing views between the CIA and the Department of Defense on the one hand, and the State Department on the other, the invasion plan was revised on more than one occasion and did not result in a well coordinated, coherent campaign. Apparently torn between his advisors and plagued by his concern for public opinion, President Kennedy wavered in his resolve. In hindsight, the Bay of Pigs has been described as a "calamity, in the measure that it fortified the notion of American inability to use its power without paralyzing inhibitions about world opinion."[14]

Of the 1,200 men who participated in the invasion, 80 were killed and 1,122 captured after 72 hours of fighting.[15] The prisoners were subjected to the most inhuman conditions for over eighteen months. Several of them are reported to have become mentally ill and one attempted suicide.[16] Following their capture, Castro proposed to release the prisoners in exchange for five hundred bulldozers. In May of 1961, the Kennedy administration declined to take part in such negotiations; however, later, it engaged in private discussions and arranged for private contributions of almost $30 million and federal income tax incentives of about $20 million for the cash ransom and purchase of commodities that resulted in the release of the remaining prisoners in December of 1962.[17]

Following the Bay of Pigs, the Kennedy Administration is reported to have initiated "a program of terror, sabotage and economic embargo, specifically designed to make it impossible for the Cuban government to continue in power."[18] The "terror" and "sabotage" portion of the program were embodied in Operation Mongoose. This operation is credited with numerous covert acts ranging from the contamination of Cuban sugar to attempts to assassinate Castro.[19]

Meanwhile, the Soviet Union was encouraged to pursue further military and economic involvement in Cuba. Castro declared himself a Marxist-Leninist in December of 1961 and US policy is revised to focus on the economic isolation of the Cuban regime. By March of 1962, the US trade embargo was extended to a total embargo except for food and medicine and included all Cuban imports and re-export of US products to Cuba from other countries. In October of 1962, the administration closed US ports to nations allowing their ships to carry arms to Cuba on ships owned by companies that traded with Cuba.[20]

By July of 1962, the Soviets were sending large shipments to Cuba that were subsequently identified as surface-to-air missiles by U-2 reconnaissance flights. The Soviet military build up continued and on October 22, President Kennedy made a public announcement of the nuclear build up in Cuba.[21] Five days later, the conflict was resolved with the Soviet Union agreeing to remove the missiles and the US agreeing not to invade Cuba.[22] There are many who believe "the crisis would not have occurred if

Washington had been prepared to tolerate the Castro regime in Cuba" [23] and that US covert action the Bay of Pigs and the economic embargo "drove the Castro regime into taking arms from the Soviet Union [and] into accepting the development of missile sites on Cuban territory."[24]

Indeed, if the US had been willing to tolerate Castro's regime in Cuba, these events may not have occurred. If the US had accepted the expropriation of US property in Cuba and the proliferation of "Castroism" throughout Latin America and the Third World, these things may not have occurred. However, Castro knew his goals would place him in conflict with the US and that he needed a like-minded ally to provide for his defense. This assertion is proven by the fact that Castro was outraged by what he perceived was the Soviet's betrayal in removing the missiles from Cuba without even consulting him.[25] After all, he had been anticipating and actively pursuing Soviet missile defense since July of 1960.[26] The Cuban Missile Crisis was a blow to Castro's ego; however, he was the ultimate victor. Contrary to the precepts of the Monroe Doctrine, the US accepted a communist regime 90 miles from its shore and Castro was placed on "life support" for nearly thirty years at a cost of about $100 billion dollars to the Soviet Union.[27]

Operation Mongoose was terminated following the Missile Crisis and a Cuba Coordinating Committee was established in the State Department to manage covert activities. The group's efforts shifted from providing support to external forces to establishing a network inside Cuba to cripple the economy and promote social unrest. In February and July of 1963, the administration extended economic sanctions making it illegal for US citizens to do business with Cuba and freezing all Cuban-owned assets in the US. A clear paradox of the Kennedy administration was that in the face of continued covert activity, on 17 November 1963, President Kennedy is reported to have met with a

French journalist and to have given him the following message for Castro:

> I think that there is not a country in the whole world, including all the regions of Africa and including any country under colonial domination, where the economic colonization, the humiliation, the exploitation have been worse than those which ravaged Cuba, the result, in part, of the policy of my country, during the regime of Batista. I think that we have spawned, constructed, entirely fabricated without knowing it, the Castro movement. I think that the accumulation of such horrors has endangered all of Latin America. Now, I will tell you something else: In a certain sense, it is as though Batista were the incarnation of some of the sins committed by the United States. Now, we must pay for those sins.[28]

President Kennedy also expressed his desire to establish relations with Cuba and to

drop the economic sanctions. The President's apologetic statement, made public after his

death, was not only in direct contrast to the actions of his administration, but also was

indicative of the non-interventionist mood that was just beginning to permeate American

society.[29]

THE JOHNSON ADMINISTRATION

The policies of the Johnson Administration (1963-1969) were not significantly

different from those of his predecessor. In moving toward the increased political and

economic isolation of Cuba, the administration adopted a two-prong approach: economic

aid to support social reform and military assistance to contain revolutionary

movements.[30] The Johnson administration was highly successful in its efforts to

internationalize the political and economic isolation of Cuba. In 1964, Brazil, Chile,

Bolivia and Uruguay had joined the list of Latin American nations that had severed

diplomatic ties with Cuba.[31] The number of voyages to Cuba by non-communist ships

decreased from 932 in 1962 to 204 in 1968 and flights reduced from 20 to one within the same time period.[32] Overall, the economic sanctions and political isolation policies of the Eisenhower, Kennedy, and Johnson administrations had a significant impact on the Cuban economy in the 1960s.

In September of 1965, in order to release some of the internal pressure, Castro announced all Cubans who wished to leave the island were free to depart from the port of Camarioca. Over 3,000[33] left Cuba through Camarioca and from 1965 to 1971, over 260,000 Cubans left Cuba via the Freedom Flights.[34] In November of 1966, President Johnson signed the Cuban Adjustment Act exempting Cubans from general US migration laws based on their classification as political refugees. In accordance with this act, Cubans who reached the US after January 1, 1959 were eligible for permanent residency after two years.[35]

By 1968, Castro was forced to ration petroleum and sugar and launched the Great Revolutionary Offensive culminating in the nationalization of the remaining private sector and mobilization of the population for agricultural production. The state of the economy forced Castro to temporarily abandon his revolutionary goals in favor of a rapprochement with the Soviet Union that would result in additional economic aid. The price of rapprochement was Castro's support of the Soviet invasion of Czechoslovakia (1968), Cuba's participation in the World Conference of Communist Parties (1972), and Cuba's membership to the Eastern European Council for Mutual Economic Assistance (1972).[36]

THE NIXON ADMINISTRATION

President Nixon and Castro were mutually distrustful and Castro "feared that as the war in Vietnam came to an end, Nixon might turn against Cuba."[37] Therefore, following the President Nixon's inauguration, Cuban-Soviet relations "entered a period of close collaboration and friendliness".[38] In January of 1969, the US was in economic recession and faced increasing economic competition from Europe and Japan. The Vietnam War and the Organization of Petroleum Exporting Countries (OPEC) oil embargo of 1973 significantly impacted the political and economic policies of the US. Additionally, the administration faced the insurgence of nationalist movements in Latin America, declining prestige in the international community and a decidedly non-interventionist domestic posture.

In order to reverse these trends, and sustain the US' political and economic position, the Nixon administration employed a three-phase approach: the globalization of US banks to give the US the ability to mobilize support of US policy objectives via multi-lateral institutions; the expansion of global military alliances to promote stability via increased arms sales and military to military contacts; and the continued support of covert actions against regimes hostile to US interests.[39]

In its second term, the Nixon administration continued to focus on the political and economic isolation of Cuba and the "containment" of communism. However, as "containment" gave way to "détente", critics of the US' Cuba policy and members of the American press, grew increasingly vocal and persistent. In spite of Nixon's public stance toward the Castro regime, in 1973, the US and Cuba signed an anti-hijacking agreement The Nixon administration resisted pressure to broaden the scope of anti-hijacking negotiations to include cultural exchanges and political relations.[40] However, world events were eroding the administration's resolve. Between 1973 and 1975, Cuba's political and economic isolation within Latin America began to crumble. Peru and Chile had resumed relations and others were following suit.[41]

This shift in Latin American policy was primarily due to the fact that, beginning in 1968; Castro altered his approach in supporting revolutionary movements. He ceased attempts to export the Cuban revolutionary model opting to support nationalist regimes that took economic and political measures challenging the US. Thus, his Latin American neighbors were no longer leery of "Cubanization" efforts and were increasingly drawn to restore relations.

Finally, Nixon's China policy was perceived as a paradox vis-à-vis his stand on communist regimes. Its critics questioned the administration's rapprochement to China in light of its isolationist policy toward Cuba. Although the administration maintained its public position that any re-examination of the Cuba policy would be predicated by a change in Castro's relationship with the Soviet Union, Latin America and the US, a month before President Nixon resigned, a secret message was transmitted between Secretary of State Kissinger and Castro to determine if there was a climate for change.[42]

THE FORD ADMINISTRATION

The Ford Administration did not publicly depart from the established isolationist policy. However, in September of 1974, two senators were allowed to visit Cuba and, at their request, Castro released four political prisoners. A month later, the Ford Administration sent a second message to Castro on arrangements for secret discussions to identify points of conflict between the two countries and to explore possible solutions.[43] These discussions involved Assistant Secretary of State William Rogers, Assistant to the

99

Secretary of State Lawrence Eagleburger and, Ramon Sanchez Parodi, Castro's envoy from the America's Department of the Communist Party. Meetings were held between November of 1974 and November of 1975. Meanwhile, the US Senate established a bipartisan committee to investigate the CIA's foreign and domestic operations (January 1975) and the US voted with 15 nations to lift Organization of American States (OAS) sanctions against Cuba (March 1975).[44]

By 1975, Castro believed the US was not an obstacle to his revolutionary ideals. He was confident the US' withdrawal from Vietnam, its preoccupation with reasserting its economic supremacy and the Watergate scandal had crippled US resolve making it unwilling or unable to oppose his incursions.[45] In October of 1975, Cuba deployed 35,000 troops to Angola[46] in support of the incumbent socialist regime. In December, President Ford declared Cuba's involvement in Angola and support of the Puerto Rican independence movement precluded the possibility of restoring diplomatic relations. Sixteen months later, another secret meeting was held to continue negotiations started in November of 1975 on family visitations.[47]

THE CARTER ADMINISTRATION

During the Carter administration, the rapprochement that began in the last month of the Nixon administration gained significant momentum. The overriding philosophy of the administration was that "political and economic ties with the United States might moderate Cuban behavior....[or] provide instruments for U.S. leverage which were otherwise denied to Washington in the absence of U.S.- Cuban linkages."[48] Several of the officials in the Carter administration had served on the Commission on United States-

Latin American Relations that in 1975 had recommended a change in Cuba policy. The Commission which based its recommendation on the changes in Cuba, Latin America and the international community, did not believe the US' policy of isolation served its national interest. It referenced the US' accommodation of the Soviet Union and China, the increasing isolation of the US vis-à-vis Latin America; and the international community and the inefficiency of the economic embargo. In general, the Carter administration adopted an anti-Cold War approach to foreign policy de-emphasizing hemispheric security issues. Thus, it moved quickly to remove obstacles to rapprochement with Cuba.[49]

In March of 1977, the administration cancelled reconnaissance flights over Cuba, dropped the ban on travel and reduced restrictions on the spending of money in Cuba. It also entered into discussions on terrorism (April 1977), concluded a fishing rights and maritime boundaries agreement (April 1977), and in May of 1977, the US and Cuba established Interest Sections in each other's capitals. Nevertheless, core differences remained unresolved.[50]

Again, in April of 1977, Castro sent 200 Cubans trainers to support the Katangan Rebellion and deployed troops to the Congo, Mozambique, Guinea, Ginea-Bissau and Equitorial Guinea. In January of 1978, Castro deployed 20,000 troops to Ethiopia. In February, Secretary of State Cyrus Vance declared Cuba's presence in Angola made it impossible to pursue the normalization of relations. A year later, Cuba sponsored the overthrow of the Samoza regime in Nicaragua and the temporary establishment of a Marxist government in Grenada.[51]

Between 1970 and 1975, Cuba experienced moderate economic growth due to abnormally high sugar prices and its ability to purchase oil from the Soviet Union at less than OPEC prices.[52] Thus, with the help of the Soviet Union, Castro was able to finance this revolutionary ventures emerging from the 1970s as the leader of the nonaligned movement.[53] However in 1976, sugar prices plummeted and, by 1980, it became necessary for Castro to release internal pressure. Thus, on April 22, 1980, Castro announced anyone wishing to leave Cuba could depart from Mariel and 123,000 Cubans migrated to the US. Several of the immigrants were criminals, mentally ill patients, and those deemed socially unacceptable.[54]

In May of 1980, the Carter administration demanded the Cuban government impose and orderly departure and established a blockade to prevent private citizens from traveling to Cuba to pick up refugees. The exodus ended in September and three months later, the US and Cuba initiated discussion on the repatriation of the "Marielitos". The Mariel exodus clearly illustrates a policy of "procrastination"[55] and "paralysis"[56] in the first month of the invasion. In the 1980s and early 1990s, Castro opposed the Soviet Union's move to Perestroika (Restructuring) and Glasnost (Political Opening). In Cuba, Castro increased economic regimentation and called for greater sacrifice from the people.[57]

THE REAGAN ADMINISTRATION

The Reagan administration is credited with the resurgence of national pride. The fiasco of the Bay of Pigs, the social upheaval of the Vietnam War, the economic crisis of the early 1970s, the Watergate scandal, and the embarrassment of the Iranian hostage crisis ended and the US entered a period of optimism and self-confidence. In order to protect US interests, particularly the two-thirds of the US trade and oil shipments that passed through the Panama Canal and the Caribbean Sea, the administration increased its military and non-military aid to Latin America and launched its Caribbean Base Initiative program.[58] The Reagan administration's Cuba policy can be classified into four periods: confrontation (1981-1984), bilateral negotiations (1984-1985), increased confrontation (1985-1987) and return to bilateral negotiations (1987-1988). [59]

The early years of the Reagan administration were reminiscent of the 1960s and early 1970s. The administration re-energized earlier commitments to regional and global diplomatic and economic sanctions backed by the threat of military force under the "carrot and stick"[60] leadership of Secretary of State, Alexander Haig. This, coupled with a concern for Cuba's ties to the Soviet Union and its support of Third World nationalist and revolutionary movements, resulted in a major effort to rollback revolutionary gain in Latin America and to seek major foreign policy concessions from US allies. In spite of the administrations stance, meetings were held in November of 1981 (Cuban Vice President and the Secretary of State) and March of 1982 (Castro and Gen Vernon Walters) to discuss the situation in Central America; however, these talks were not pursued further.[61]

In October of 1983, the US military intervened in Grenada in support of the Organization of Eastern Caribbean States in order to restore order following the assassination of leftist leader Maurice Bishop. From the US, perspective, the intervention was prompted by concern for the safety of American students in Grenada and the discovery that the Cubans had built a runway long enough to support Soviet MIG and refueling operations. Additionally, during the intervention, US troops uncovered tons of military equipment and intelligence assessments validating the Soviets and Cubans had been building an arsenal that could have been used against governments throughout the Caribbean. [62]

During the first bilateral negotiation period, the administration concluded a migration agreement providing for the repatriation of "Marielitos", US admission of 3,000 political prisoners, and the immigration of 20,000 Cubans on an annual basis. In January of 1985, a delegation of US bishops traveled to Cuba and secured the release of 44 prisoners.[63] In the period of increased confrontation, the administration launched Radio Marti and signed a trade act eliminating restrictions on the export of books, films and records to and from Cuba. In turn, Cuba abrogated the 1984 immigration agreement (re-established in 1987). In the same period, in 1986, the Treasury Department announced measures to tighten the embargo to include a crackdown on trading with Cuban-front companies in Panama, controls on organizations promoting travel to Cuba, lower limits on cash and gifts sent to Cuba by exiled relatives and tighter controls on companies shipping food and care packages from Cuban-Americans to relatives in Cuba.[64]

In its last year, the Reagan administration returned to bilateral negotiations and several meetings were held to discuss nuclear issues, Angola and radio frequency disputes. The international climate was changing and relations between the US and the Soviet Union were improving. Domestically, the Iran-Contra affair undermined the integrity of the US' political system and the State Department as well as liberal elements in Congress increasingly asserted their influence over Cuba policy. [65]

THE BUSH ADMINISTRATION

The Bush administration, in contrast to the Nixon, Ford, and Reagan administrations, internalized the pre-conditions for rapprochement between the two nations. Much to Castro's dismay, the administration pre-conditioned normalization of relations on Cuba's adopting democratic reforms to include: free and supervised elections, respect for human rights, freedom for Cubans to travel abroad, and the end to foreign revolutionary subversion. The administration also applied economic assistance measures to isolate the regime from US allies as well as Eastern Europe, the Soviet Union, and China. In September of 1991, the Soviet Union announced the withdrawal of all Soviet military personnel and economic assistance was established on the basis of non-subsidized trade. The barter of oil for sugar was terminated and weapons sales scheduled to be phased out.[66]

When the Soviet Union collapsed in December of 1991, Cuba lost approximately $4 to $6 billion of annual support.[67] These measures crippled the Cuban economy, which had shrunk by and estimated 35% to 50% between 1989 and 1993.[68] In February of 1992, the US Congress passed the "Cuban Democracy Act." The bill established sanctions against countries assisting Cuba, increased restriction on aid, permitted direct telephone service between the US and Cuba, prohibited vessels that visited Cuban ports from entering US ports and restricted remittances to Cuba. In accordance with this act, certain provisions can be waived if Cuba agrees to specific conditions to include free elections.[69]

The US' Cuba policy, since 1952, is most aptly described by Professor Irving Louis Horowitz as "paradox followed by procrastination, ending in paralysis."[70] During the

Eisenhower administration, the misinformation at all levels and the rift between the Department of State on the one hand, and the Department of Defense and the Central Intelligence Agency on the other, were contributing factors to the policy paradox. Even after the key players were convinced the agrarian farmer was a threat to US business interests, and a potential threat to the US national security, they failed to develop a coherent plan to, at a minimum, limit the damage.[71]

The Kennedy administration was not impaired by misinformation; however, the schism between its key advisors seriously impacted the formulation of a coherent policy. There is also some evidence that the Kennedy administration's policy was affected by the President's personal dichotomy on the issue of Cuba. That is, some of his statements reflect a sense of culpability and guilt for the manner in which the US had historically approached US-Cuba relations and, to some extent, respect for Castro's nationalistic revolution.[72] On the other hand, his official position and action, until the last months of his presidency, reflected a desire to affect the demise of the Castro regime.[73]

In the Johnson administration, US policy shifted from a unilateral, internal policy to a multi-lateral, external policy. Covert actions and economic sanctions to depose the regime from within were abandoned in favor of multi-lateral economic actions to obtain support for the containment of Communism throughout Latin America and Castroism in Cuba. However, the Vietnam War made the malaise that resulted from the Bay of Pigs and the Cuban Missile Crisis worse and both the Johnson and Nixon administrations had to contend with the nation's move toward political isolationism. US policy was increasingly influenced by the rejection of "Monroeism"[74] and an increasing number of "apologists"[75] who bemoaned colonial and imperialist subjugation while refusing "to examine the interstices of the most totalitarian regime in the history of Latin America."[76] In this regard, the Johnson administration's Cuba policy embarked upon the path of procrastination.

The Ford administration was the first administration to allow members of government to visit Cuba since diplomatic relations were severed in 1961. [77] Although the administration's official position did not depart from the isolationist policy of the latter part of the Nixon administration, the "paradox"[78] between its public and private policy was, to a large extent, attributable to the continued influence of Dr. Henry Kissinger. In 1975, Dr. Kissinger saw "no virtue in perpetual antagonism between the United States and Cuba"[79] and was prepared to move the US "in a new position if Cuba did."[80] If Castro had not sent troops to Angola and supported the Puerto Rican independence movement, the Ford administration may have continued to explore a rapprochement with Cuba.

By far, the Carter administration contributed more than any other toward a rapprochement with Cuba. However, as was the case during the Ford administration, Castro interpreted US overtures as signs of weakness that fueled his revolutionary incursions into Africa and Latin America. The Mariel exodus of 1980 introduced the element that would, from this point on, place US policy in what appears to be a perpetual state of "paralysis."[81]

The Reagan administration focused on re-establishing US pre-eminence in Latin America via hemispheric military assistance and economic assistance programs. Undoubtedly, the administration was successful in asserting its position vis-à-vis Cuba via the Grenada incursion. However, the issue of the return of the Mariel detainees mitigated its actions and the Iran-Contra affair weakened its political resolve in the last year of the administration. The Bush administration attempted to capitalize on the demise of the Soviet Union and Cuba's resulting economic crisis; however, the migration crises of 1990 and 1994 tempered the administration's stance toward Cuba.

The Clinton administration actually had very little reason and, perhaps due to the President's experience with the Mariel detainees in Arkansas, very little desire to get involved in Cuban affairs. In any event, when Castro released yet another wave of Cubans in 1994, the administration was forced to deal with the problem of Cuban migration. At this point, the administration began to focus on "people-to-people" programs as a go-around to help the Cuban people without helping the Cuban government. Ultimately, the goal was to improve the quality of life of the Cuban people in order to deter them from migrating to the US. Castro interpreted the people-to-people measures as regime de-stabilizers and relations took a turn for the worse with the shoot-down of the Brothers to the Rescue aircraft in 1996. The resulting Helms-Burton Act was an aberration for the Clinton administration, which, like the Carter administration, would prefer to pursue rapprochement with the Cuban government.

US policy transitioned from the covert, political, and economic measures to affect the demise of the Castro regime to economic and political isolation, containment and finally, stasis. Attempts to covertly or economically depose the Castro regime began to wither away with the Bay of Pigs fiasco as US policy shifted from "paradox" to "procrastination" and died in the aftermath of the Vietnam War. The covert actions and political and economic isolationist policies of the 1960s gave way to an effort to contain

"Castroism." However, containment turned out to be a political euphemism and did not serve to contain those who want the right to control their lives and their destinies.

Thus, the migration crises of 1980, 1990 and 1994, brought more of "them" (the Cubans) here. These large migrations had significant impact on the socio-economic systems and shocked policy makers into a state of political stasis or paralysis. Notwithstanding, in growing numbers, "they" are "us" and a coherent policy must be developed to ensure that when, not if, the time comes, the US is prepared to provide for its national security and to act in the best interest of all of its citizens and their families to include the family members who are currently living on the island of Cuba.

Before turning to a proposal for a process whereby US policy makers can develop a viable Cuba policy, it is appropriate to review the policy of the Clinton administration and the scenarios for political change in Cuba that may affect the current policy.

Notes

[1] Morley, 330.

[2] Simons, 292.

[3] Simons, 292.

[4] Simons, 293.

[5] John F. Kennedy; quoted in Phillip W. Bonsal, *Castro and the United States.*

[6] John F. Kennedy; quoted in Phillip W. Bonsal, *Castro and the United States.*

[7] Bonsal, 294.

[8] Suchlicki, *Columbus to Castro,* 163-165.

[9] Suchlicki, *Columbus to Castro,* 163-165.

[10] Lazo, 269-272.

[11] Lazo, 269-272.

[12] Lazo, 295.

[13] Lazo, 297-300.

[14] Lazo, 267.

[15] US Cuba Commission, "US-Cuba History," [on-line accessed on February 7, 2000], available from http://uscubacommission.org/history/html; Internet.

[16] Lazo, 320.

[17] Lazo, 313-318.

[18] Simons, 298.

[19] Simons, 299-301.

[20] "US-Cuba History."

[21] Lazo, 336.

[22] Suchlicki, 169.

[23] Simons, 315.

[24] Simons, 315.

[25] Simons, 315.

[26] Suarez, 163.

[27] "US-Cuba History."

[28] Lazo, 94.

[29] Irving Louis Horowitz, *"American Foreign Policy Toward Castro's Cuba: Paradox, Procrastination, and Paralysis,"* in *The Conscience of Worms and the Cowardice of Lions* (New Brunswick: Transaction Publishers, 1992), 4.

[30] Morley, 680.

[31] Morley, 619.

[32] Morley, 683.

[33] "US-Cuba History."

[34] "US-Cuba History."

[35] "US-Cuba History."

[36] Suchlicki, *Columbus to Castro,* 173-174.

[37] Suchlicki, *Columbus to Castro,* 174.

Notes

[38] Suchlicki, *Columbus to Castro* 174.

[39] Morley, 799-808.

[40] Morley 832.

[41] Roger W. Fontaine, *On Negotiating with Cuba* (Washington D.C: American Enterprise Institute for Public Policy Research., 1975), 52.

[42] "US-Cuba History."

[43] Morley, 833.

[44] "US-Cuba History."

[45] Suchlicki, *Columbus to Castro* 178.

[46] "US-Cuba History."

[47] "US-Cuba History."

[48] Edward Gonzalez, *A Strategy for Dealing with Cuba in the 1980s* (Santa Monica: RAND Corporation, 1992), 26.

[49] Morley, 868-872.

[50] "US-Cuba History."

[51] "US-Cuba History."

[52] Morley, 849.

[53] Suchlicki, *Columbus to Castro*, 206-208.

[54] "US-Cuba History."

[55] Horowitz, *"Paradox, Procrastination, and Paralysis,"* 4.

[56] Howitz, *"Paradox, Procrastination, and Paralysis,"* 4.

[57] Suchlicki, *Columbus to Castro*, 121.

[58] Gonzalez, *"A Strategy for Dealing with Cuba in the 1980s,"* 97.

[59] Nelson P. Valdes, *"Balance of Failure: US-Cuba Relations, 1959-1993"* (Discussion Document presented the Council on Foreign Relations, October 28, 1993) [on-line accessed February 7, 2000],available from http://www.cubanet.org/; Internet.

[60] Gonzalez, *"A Strategy for Dealing with Cuba in the 1980s,"* 30.

[61] "US-Cuba History."

[62] Kenneth N. Skoug, Jr., *The United States and Cuba Under Reagan and Shultz* (Westport: Praeger Press, 1996), 44.

[63] "US-Cuba History."

[64] "US-Cuba History."

[65] Valdes, *"Balance of Failure: US-Cuba Relations, 1959-1993."*

[66] Valdes, *"Balance of Failure: US-Cuba Relations, 1959-1993."*

[67] Mark P. Sullivan, *"Cuba: Issues for Congress"*, October 29, 1999 (Congressional Research Service (CRS): The Library of Congress, 1999), CRS-1.

[68] "US-Cuba History."

[69] "US-Cuba History."

[70] Horowitz, *"Paradox, Procrastination, and Paralysis,"* 4.

[71] Lazo, 135-156.

[72] Lazo, 94.

[73] Morley, 540-555.

[74] Horowitz, *"Paradox, Procrastination, and Paralysis,"* 5.

Notes

[75] Irving Louis Horowitz, *"The Conscience of Castrologists: Thirty-Three Years of Solitudes"* in *The Conscience of Worms and the Cowardice of Lions* (New Brunswick: Transaction Publishers, 1992), 27.

[76] Horowitz, *"The Conscience of Castrologists: Thirty-Three Years of Solitudes,"* 27.
[77] "US-Cuba History."
[78] Horowitz, *"Procrastination, and Paralysis,"* 5.
[79] Fontaine, 65.
[80] Fontaine, 65.
[81] Horowitz, *"Procrastination, and Paralysis,"* 5.

PART VI

CURRENT CUBA POLICY AND SCENARIOS FOR CHANGE IN CUBA

THE CLINTON ADMINISTRATION

The Clinton administration's Cuba policy within the confines of the Cuban Democracy and Helms Burton Acts has officially focused on migration issues and "people-to-people" outreach measures to alleviate the plight of the Cuban people and "help them prepare for a democratic future."[1]

Following Castro's declaration of an open migration policy in August of 1994, the US Cost Guard was ordered to establish a "picket line" to prevent sea-borne migrations and meetings were held that resulted in agreement "to direct Cuban migration into safe, legal and orderly channels"[2] in accordance with the 1984 migration accords. The 1994 joint communiqué established a minimum migration of 20,000 Cubans a year and, under the terms of a 1995 '"companion agreement,"[3] the US agreed to return Cubans interdicted at sea (dry feet) who could not substantiate a fear of personal persecution.[4]

In October of 1995, President Clinton announced measures to expand "people-to-people" contacts between the US and Cuba and to allow US Non-Governmental Organizations (NGOs) to pursue projects in Cuba.[5] A month later, Concilio Cuba, a Cuban NGO was formed to organize the first human rights conference in Cuba. The

Cuban government denied Concilio legal recognition and began to harass, interrogate and arrest over 200 of its leaders.[6]

On February 24, 1996, Cuban fighters shot down two Cessnas over the Florida straights resulting in the death of four Cuban-Americans who were members of the group Brothers to the Rescue. The group was primarily engaged in the humanitarian search of Cubans fleeing the island on rafts, but had also flown missions over Cuba to drop leaflets. On this occasion, they are alleged to have filed a false flight plan and to have flown over Cuba. Cuba's downing of the two planes led President Clinton to temporarily suspend all charter flights to Cuba (overturned in March of 1998), to impose travel restrictions on Cuban diplomats and to limit visits of Cuban officials to the US.

In response to this incident, the US passed the Helms-Burton or LIBERTAD Act on March 12, 1996.[7] The LIBERTAD Act contains a variety of measures to increase pressure on Cuba and provides a plan to assist Cuba in its transition to democracy. Title One codifies all existing embargo orders and regulations and there is no provision for a Presidential waiver of the embargo provisions. Titles Three and Four are the most contentious. Title Three enables US citizens to sue persons who "traffic in property confiscated in Cuba"[8] in US court. However, this has never been done due to the fact that, President Clinton has, in accordance with the provisions of this title, delayed implementation for six months at a time in the interest of expediting Cuba's transition to democracy. Under Title IV, foreign nationals involved in the confiscation of US property in Cuba or in trafficking of US property nationalized by the government of Cuba, are not admitted entry into the US. This provision can only be waived for humanitarian medical or the event those affected are required to appear in US courts regarding confiscated property. [9] As of October of 1999, the provisions of the Helms-Burton Act have been applied to a number of executives and their families those of a Mexican telecommunications company, an Israeli-owned citrus company and a Canadian mining company. [10] Titles Three and Four have drawn much criticism from the United Nations, the European Union (EU) and the OAS because they are alleged to impede on the sovereignty of foreign nations by establishing the US as the authority for determining who nations can and cannot trade with.

In response to the Helms-Burton Act, the Cuban government enacted the Law Reaffirming Cuban Dignity and Sovereignty (1996) implemented via the Law of Protection of the Independence and the Cuban Economy, which took effect in March of 1999. The combined effect of these laws is to "impose harsh penalties for up to twenty years for any actions that could be interpreted as support for the US embargo on Cuba." [11]

Toward the latter part of 1996, the Clinton administration took steps to obtain support for its Cuba "democratization" policies [12] and in the same year, the EU adopted the "Common Position on Cuba" [13] conditioning developmental assistance to Cuba on democratic change. [14] In January of 1997, President Clinton released the report on the assistance the US and the international community would provide a transition government in Cuba and in April of 1997, the rift between the US and the EU caused by the provisions of the LIBERTAD Act, were partially resolved when both countries agreed to suspend the legal case against the legislation and to pursue a combined effort to deter investment in confiscated property. [15]

Following Pope John Paul's visit to Cuba in 1998, President Clinton announced four changes in US policy: the resumption of licensing for flights to Cuba; the resumption of remittances up to $300 per quarter for relatives; the intent to streamline and expedite licensing procedures for the sale of medicines and to work with Congress on the transfer of food to Cuba. These measures were expanded by the President in 1995 as follows: to allow US residents to send up to $300 a quarter to anyone in Cuba not just relatives; to allow for licensing of larger remittances by US citizens and American NGOs to Cuban NGOs; to expand direct charter flights from cities other than Miami and to other than Cuba; to re-establish direct mail service; to authorize the sale of food to Cuban private businesses and to expand "people-to-people" contacts.[16]

To date, the efforts of the administration, which will be analyzed in greater detail in the following part, have focused primarily on "people-to-people" measures intended to support the Cuban people in a transition to democracy. The administration's efforts to affect political change of the existing system have, in the short-term, not been successful. In order to succeed in the long-term, the "people-to-people" measures would have to empower Cuba's embryonic civil society enabling its members to pursue political and economic reforms. Moreover, a proactive long-term policy would have to consider all scenarios that may affect US-Cuban relations prepared contingency plans that would lead to proactive vice reactive courses of action.

In 1991, several people proclaimed the imminent fall of the Castro regime. Nearly ten years later, they are still waiting. Castro was able to survive the economic chaos that accompanied the demise of the Soviet Union; however, short of his inevitable death, there are also several scenarios that may lead to the fall of the Castro regime.

SCENARIOS FOR POLITICAL CHANGE IN CUBA

There have been numerous scenarios developed for Cuba's transition to democracy as well as the demise of the Castro regime. Those developed by Edward Gonzalez are particularly useful in analyzing the ramifications changes in Cuban affairs are likely to have on the US' national security, national interest, and its Cuba policy. Gonzalez developed four "endgames" or scenarios based on the assumption that, "first, US policy remains in force [and] second, the regime continues to move toward a "Marxist-Leninist" model in which there is partial, state-directed economic liberalization combined with authoritarian rule."[17]

In the first scenario, the regime operating in a "controlled crisis situation….muddles through and survives."[18] This scenario basically describes the status quo in Cuba. The regime is in complete control via the repressive measures of its security agencies. The economy is on "life support" due to modest economic gains derived from foreign investment, tourism and exile remittances. There is no civil society to speak of and therefore, no political opposition. Also, the country's economic development is stifled by Castro's "politization" of the economic system. Therefore, the socio-economic environment postulated in this scenario could deteriorate due to a poor sugar harvest, a natural disaster or some as yet unforeseen political event.

The US has been experiencing the ramifications of this scenario for about the last twenty years. Due to Castro's repressive control of the Cuban people, Cuba has been "less disruptive to the rest of the Caribbean and [poses] fewer problems to US interests."[19] However, developments over the last two decades have shown Cuba continues to pose a security risk due to "the prospect of future illegal migrant surges, the island's potential as a major transshipment base for illegal drug trafficking, and the possible eruption of widespread civil disorder on the island."[20] The stagnation of the economy and the waves of political repression continue to force Cubans to sacrifice their lives to survive the ninety-mile voyage that brings them to the US. By July of 1999, nearly 3,000 Cubans had been interdicted at sea or seashore for that year as compared to little over 2,000 in calendar year 1998.[21]

Additionally, there is considerable evidence to support that fact that the government of Cuba has supported and actively participated in trafficking activity via the use of its airspace since the early 1960s.[22] Beginning, in 1982, "a sufficient body of evidence [had] been reported and compiled by government agencies, grand juries, informants and defectors to unmistakably tie Cuba to the drug trade."[23] In the Fall of 1999, a 7.2-ton shipment of Columbian cocaine allegedly destined for Spain via Cuba was confiscated in the Caribbean port of Cartagena. The cocaine was found in containers "consigned to a firm in Havana that manufactured plastic figurines for export to Europe."[24]

The firm involved was a foreign venture formed by two Spaniards and a Cuban government enterprise and, although Cuban authorities provided the information on the final destination of the narcotics shipment, they insisted the investigation did not disclose any Cuban involvement. However, the plot thickens as, in December, a Columbian witness was shot in his country and the owner of the Cuban firm suspected involved in the deal, his wife and son, were shot and killed in Cuba. Additionally, in March of this year, the Federal Bureau of Investigation issued an arrest warrant for Victor Tafur, the son of a former Senator who was allegedly killed in 1992 for his role in drafting the US-Columbian extradition legislation.[25] In November of 1999, President Clinton failed to

118

place Cuba on the list of nations trafficking in narcotics[26]; however, as long as the Cuban economy remains in crisis, drug trafficking will continue to be a low-cost, low-risk option for Castro to remain in power.

Unquestionably, with the exception of the political chaos that results from the graft and corruption associated with narcotics traffic in Columbia, the region has been relatively stable. However, recent events in Venezuela and Ecuador point to the political volatility of Latin America and the potential dangers of complacency on the part of the US.

Given the assumptions, made in this scenario, US policy would not change; however, "stability would depend on the regime's ability to maintain a tight lid on the populace….[and] the possibility would always exist that an unanticipated spark…could cause a popular explosion."[27] In the absence of a contingency plan, US policy makers would have no recourse but to develop a reactive plan that would, at best, take care of the immediate crisis.

The second scenario, "heightened authoritarianism and stasis"[28] develops when "economic and political conditions worsen [and] Cuba is plunged into an uncontrolled crisis situation. Much of the island, especially Havana experiences political unrest and violence of a greater magnitude than occurred with the riots in August 1994."[29] In this scenario, there is rapid escalation of civil disobedience and mass demonstrations, strikes and riots that result in the mobilization of the island's security agencies. Order is restored by the Revolutionary Armed Forces (FAR) and "with the FAR institutionally dominant and hardliners in control, Cuban society [becomes] increasingly militarized and political dissent [is] even more repressed." As a result of the government's crackdown, "foreign investment [dries] up along with tourism."[30] Meanwhile, "migration pressures…greatly intensify"[31] leading to increased tension between Cuba and the US. The Cuban government's "reliance on open, heavy-handed coercion [accelerates] regime delegitimation in the eyes of the civilian populace"[32] and "within the ranks of the FAR itself."[33] If viewed as a stand-alone proposition, this scenario would result in the militarization of the economy and society and lead to "stasis in the reform process."[34] However, if the government were unable to de-mobilize society and the military were unable to produce the required economic reforms, the external political pressure would "set the stage for other endgames that also involve uncontrolled crisis situations."[35]

This scenario is likely to present itself upon the death of Fidel Castro. It is probable that his death will initially result in a migration exodus several times larger than in 1980, 1990, and 1994. Thousands upon thousands of Cubans are likely to take to the seas in the initial confusion simply because they would not know what to expect. Those who flee would probably have relatives in the US or Europe. On the other hand, those left behind would experience the effects of a deteriorating economy as the exile remittances dwindle and the tourist economy suffers due to the social and political turbulence. If Raul Castro were to assume control, the government would respond with a rapid and military "offensive" that would lead to a violent confrontation of Cubans against Cubans.

Invariably, this would de-legitimize the government and cause members of the FAR to "defect" as an act of conscience in lieu of participating in armed conflict against fellow Cubans. If and when the government regained control, it would face unprecedented pressure to reform from within and from its foreign investors. The management of the foreign investment ventures would most likely, as Gonzalez suggests, become the responsibility of the military elite. However, if the military leaders were unable to stabilize the political climate or, if they were to employ excessive violence in the process of restoring order, they would draw international criticism and ultimately jeopardize foreign business ventures.

Internationally, the news media would draw attention to human rights abuses and apply pressure on the US and its allies to alleviate the plight of those suffering at the hands of the military in Cuba. If the government failed to restore stability and demobilize the society, this scenario would lead to foreign (US or coalition) intervention. On the other hand, if the government were able to restore order and to establish a participative dialogue to initiate reform, this scenario could develop into a modified version of Gonzalez' third "endgame", "non-violent change and power sharing."[36]

As envisioned by Gonzalez, the third scenario, "non-violent change and power sharing,"[37] results from "the economy's sharp deterioration [which] produces growing anti-regime opposition among the populace at large"[38] and "division within the regime [which sharpens] as civilian reformers split with the hardliners, centrists, and Castro brothers."[39] This scenario assumes that "at some point in this endgame Fidel Castro is no longer around leaving a momentary leadership vacuum"[40] that makes it possible for the "army units under the command of progressive officers, the populace at large, [and] reformist leaders [to] seize power" and to form "a new coalition government"[41]

In order for the new coalition to survive, it would have to include a considerable number of the FAR with access to the weapons and ammunition required to resist the government's attempt to stay in power. Additionally, the coalition forces would also have to include members of the Cuban "intelligencia" to undertake the immediate political and economic reforms that would give impetus to a long-term reform movement. Another of the assumptions of this scenario is that "it would see a replacement of the Castro regime by a new government that would be market and democratically oriented, and committed to a national reconciliation and cooperation with Cuba's neighbors including the United States."[42]

The underlying assumption is that the founders of the new coalition government are "market and democratically oriented."[43] In reality, those who form the new coalition government would have been influenced by Cuban culture and nurture and its metamorphosis over the past forty-one years. The cultural and historical "baggage" will be more difficult to handle as Cuba attempts to integrate into a highly sophisticated world economy. Therefore, a dawn-day change is highly unlikely. A more realistic scenario would call for some immediate economic reforms to alleviate the island's economic plight giving impetus to a gradual and more significant political, social and economic reforms.

As envisioned, a part of this scenario is already underway. That is, Cuba's political and economic environment has experienced "sharp deterioration [producing] growing anti-regime opposition."[44] However, due to Castro's complete control over society, dissidents have been unable to develop into a "more organized and widespread"[45] opposition force. Thus, a modified version of this scenario would postulate that, a coalition government would develop as a result of internal and external pressure to reform in the aftermath of Castro's death.

If one interprets Gonzalez' first scenario or "Endgame I: The Regime Muddles Through"[46] as a description of the current situation, then "Endgame IV: Violent System

Change,"[47]may be considered a third, and the least desirable result, of Cuba's economic and political tailspin.

In this scenario, "Castro and the hardliners continue to dominate the regime."[48] Reforms are not enacted or, if they are, they are too little an too late to arrest the country's economic and political [and social] decline."[49] Whereas in the second scenario the decline results in "heightened authoritarianism and political stasis,"[50] and in the third scenario it leads to "non-violent change and power sharing,"[51] the fourth scenario results in the regime's downfall and radical system change. As a result, "Cuba is plunged into Civil War."[52] The government's opposition is formed by "a vengeful rightist movement"[53] consisting of civilians and members of the defectors from the FAR. The new government "engages in repression and outright violence against those suspected of having supported the old regime,"[54] outlaws the Communist Party, and prosecutes those who were formerly loyal to the Castro brothers.

Although the new government pledges to hold democratic elections, "there is no civil society or party system to pursue the government to restore democratic rule."[55] This scenario assumes "mass protests erupt throughout the island and cannot be contained by the regime's security forces."[56] However, events in 1994 and since have shown the government is quite capable of re-establishing order. Moreover, the underlying assumption that the people would engage in "mass protests" is highly unlikely. The dissident protests that accompanied the Ibero-American Summit in November of 1999 clearly show the limits of civil protests and the repressive efficiency of the island's security forces. Between November and December of 1999, approximately 160 people were detained and 190 people restricted from traveling within Cuba.[57] On the other hand, the assumption that the FAR would split is feasible; however, if civilian opposition was to be supported by armed defectors from the FAR, a civil war would likely ensue that would have serious impact on the United States. Faced with international and domestic pressure to intervene to curtail a mass exodus, to curtail human rights abuses and to curtail the potential deterioration of the public health, the US would inevitably be drawn in.

A rightist or militaristic government emerging from a civil war environment may be pre-disposed to defraying elections for the sake of restoring order. While either would continue to deprive the Cuban people of a constitutional government, both would eventually provide the stability desired by the international community.

In essence, the new regime would be a déjà vu of 1952 with a tougher economic challenge. Both would pursue economic reforms to assist in the process; however, if "the new government's first priority is Cuba's recovery through rapid conversion to a market economy"[58] without due consideration to the pre-requisite or complimentary political and social reforms, the benefits of short-term capital growth will be overcome by long-term inequities in capital distribution. As a stand-alone proposition, this scenario might be desirable for the US and the international community because it would effectively restore order and limit the exodus from the island; however, It would be the least desirable for the Cuban people

On the other hand, if the purpose of the rightist or militaristic opposition were to restore order and to relinquish control to a coalition government, then the Cuban people, the United States and the international community would benefit particularly if the new coalition government (Endgame III) were in a position to undertake political, economic and social reforms.

Ernesto Betancourt, a Private Consultant and former Director, Office of Cuba Broadcasting/Radio Marti, has presented similar scenarios for the inevitable end of the Castro regime."[59] Betancourt offers a scenario whereby Castro undertakes "an apocalyptic last ditch struggle against the hated Americans…to seek a place in history for himself." [60] Citing Castro's 1958 letter to Celia Cruz, Betancourt believes, "recent events, so far ignored by US officials and [the] US mainstream media, reflect a pattern that raises the plausible hypothesis that Castro is making preparations for a final provocation against the US to fulfill his *true destiny.*"[61] Betancourt asserts that events to include: the 1998 arrest of the ten spies involved in gathering information on activity and personnel assigned to a military installation in Florida; reports that Cuba has developed biological weapons and delivery systems, and Cuba's ability to interfere with US air traffic control systems, make the "apocalyptic" theory feasible. In fact, he states that although, "such a possibility is written off as incredible by rational people,"[62] the US' "lack of response so far is making [it] easier for Castro to test the various options in which he is investing significant human, material and financial resources."[63]

This scenario is regarded as highly unlikely by those who believe that all leaders are rational and base their actions on a logical decision making process guided by the greater good and an assessment of probable outcomes. However, Betancourt points out, "Castro has shown in previous crisis that he doesn't care about the sufferings he may impose on the Cuban people"[64] and that an "apocalyptic" scenario is most likely to occur if Castro believes his ability to stay in power is seriously threatened.

A rational person would never believe a leader of Castro's obvious intelligence capable of inciting atrocities for the sake of a "grand finale"; however, his reaction to the Soviet's removal of the missiles from Cuba in 1962, clearly demonstrated his resolve to stand toe-to-toe with the US and to secure his place in history as the force who opposed the US. As unlikely as one may like to believe, the possibility exists that Castro may choose to make a grand exit. Therefore, US policy should be prepared to deal with acts of provocation at the covert and political levels.

According to Edward Gonzalez and Richard Nuccio, "foreign policy generalists like to point out that Cuba occupies an inordinate amount of importance in Congress and the Executive Branch given the island's small size and lack of economic and military might."[65] In fact, due to its economic austerity, the Cuban government has downsized its armed forces and equipment inventories thereby reducing its ability to seriously threaten the security of the US. Nevertheless, its proximity to the US, its potential command of US coastal waters and its past performance on issues of migration and drug trafficking, make Cuba a volatile security risk. There is no doubt that Castro will not initiate any type of reform and that "instead, [the government] remains in both a survival and succession mode, whereby the leadership is preparing to perpetuate itself in the event that Castro dies or is incapacitated owing to failing health."[66]

Assuming the leadership is able "to perpetuate itself"[67] and to retain power and control, the impact on the US and the international community will be minimal and perhaps restricted to a limited wave of migration(s). However, in the interim, the government of the small island continues to hold US policy makers hostage to the threat of unrestricted migration that limits US response to its political provocations. Although this reality makes it appear difficult to formulate a coherent and consistent policy, the burdensome task can be simplified if US policy was developed on the three-tier approach of short-term, mid-term and long-term objectives.

In this context, the short-term objectives would focus on issues that directly impact the US' national security or national interests that could feasibly be negotiated with the Castro regime. These short-term objectives should be limited to issues for which there is hope of arriving at a short-term resolution. The immigration issue is a typical example of a short-term objective. Mid-term issues would be the subject of discussion and negotiation and would include concerns that do not directly impact US national security or interests. The mid-term issues would be those for which the US does not require or expect a short-term resolution and may involve multi-lateral negotiations. For example, foreign investment in Cuba and its impact on human rights as it pertains to violations of international labor accords. This issue does not directly impact US security; however it does support national interests upon which the US was founded.

Those issues that are known to be in direct opposition to the ideology of the Castro regime, or the government that succeeds it, should be approached as long-term objectives. Two such issues would be the establishment of free elections and the conversion to a market economy. Both issues are clearly opposed by Castro and the current leadership of the regime, which, in a peaceful transition, is likely to form the new government.

Unfortunately, "the longer Cuba's inevitable transition to a post-Castro polity and economy is delayed, the more likely it will be that the Cuban people will suffer intense violence and be ill-prepared to embark upon Cuba's reconstruction through viable

127

democratic institutions."[68] Under these circumstances, the US will inevitably be drawn in and, as it stands, ill prepared to contribute in other than a reactionary mode. In order to secure US national interests and to support the humanitarian principles upon which the country was founded, US policy makers need to develop a proactive vice reactive Cuba policy.

Notes

[1] US Interest Section, "People-to-People Fact Sheet", [on-line accessed on February 12, 2000], available at http://www.state.gov/www/regions/wha/cuba/people. html; Internet.

[2] US Interest Section, "Migration Fact Sheet," [on-line accessed on February 12, 2000], available at http://www.state.gov/www/regions/wha/cuba/people.html; Internet.

[3] "Migration Fact Sheet."

[4] "Migration Fact Sheet."

[5] David A. Mutchler, "USAID Program Mandate for Cuba," [on-line accessed 13 February 2000], available at http://www.info.usaid.gov/courntries/cu/mand.cub.htm; Internet.

[5] Sullivan, "Cuba: Issues for Congress," CRS-3.

[7] Sullivan, "Cuba: Issues for Congress," CRS-5-6.

[8] Sullivan, "Cuba: Issues for Congress," CRS-8-10.

[9] Sullivan, "Cuba: Issues for Congress," CRS-8-10.

[10] Sullivan, "Cuba: Issues for Congress," CRS-8-9.

[11] Human Rights Watch, *Cuba's Repressive Machinery: Human Rights Forty Years After the Revolution* (Human Rights Watch, June 1999) [on-line accessed March 1, 2000], available at http://www.hrw.org/hrw/reports/1999/cuba; Internet.

[12] Sullivan, "Cuba: Issues for Congress," CRS-9-10.

[13] Sullivan, "Cuba: Issues for Congress," CRS-8-10.

[14] "US-Cuba History."

[15] "US-Cuba History."

[16] "People-to-People Fact Sheet."

[17] Edward Gonzalez, *Cuba Clearing Perilous Waters?* (Santa Monica: RAND Corporation, 1996), 107.

[18] Gonzalez, *Clearing Perilous Waters?*, 107.

[19] Gonzalez, *Clearing Perilous Waters?*, 109.

[20] Phyllis Greene Walker, Edward Gonzalez, and Richard Nuccio, "U.S. Interests and Stakes in Cuban Transition Outcomes" in *The RAND Forum on Cuba*, Forum convened in Washington D.C., April 16-17, 1998, edited by Edward Gonzalez and Richard Nuccio (Santa Monica: The RAND Corporation, 1998), 16.

[21] "Migration Fact Sheet."

[22] Emilio T. Gonzalez, *The Cuban Connection: Drug Trafficking and the Castro Regime*, Cuban Studies Association, Occassional Paper Series, vol. 2, no. 6., July 15, 1997 (Cuban Studies Association, 1997),1.

[23] Gonzalez, *The Cuban Connection*,1.

[24] Juan O. Tamayo, "Deadly Twists in Colombia Drug Case Test U.S. Relations", *Miami Herald*, May 3, 2000.

[25] Tamayo, "Deadly Twists in Colombia."

[26] Frank Davies, "Anti-Drug Officials Downplay Cuba's Role in Trade", *Miami Herald*, November 18, 1999.

[27] Gonzalez, *Cuba Clearing Perilous Waters?* , 111.

[28] Gonzalez, *Cuba Clearing Perilous Waters?* , 111.

[29] Gonzalez, *Cuba Clearing Perilous Waters?*, 1996), 111.

Notes

[30] Gonzalez, *Cuba Clearing Perilous Waters?*, 113.

[31] Gonzalez, *Cuba Clearing Perilous Waters?*, 111.

[32] Gonzalez, *Cuba Clearing Perilous Waters?*, 114.

[33] Gonzalez, *Cuba Clearing Perilous Waters?*, 114.

[34] Gonzalez, *Cuba Clearing Perilous Waters?*, 112.

[35] Gonzalez, *Cuba Clearing Perilous Waters?*, 114.

[36] Gonzalez, *Cuba Clearing Perilous Waters?* , 114.

[37] Gonzalez, *Cuba Clearing Perilous Waters?* , 114.

[38] Gonzalez, *Cuba Clearing Perilous Waters?* , 114.

[39] Gonzalez, *Cuba Clearing Perilous Waters?* ,114-115.

[40] Gonzalez, *Cuba Clearing Perilous Waters?* , 115.

[41] Gonzalez, *Cuba Clearing Perilous Waters?*, 115.

[42] Gonzalez, *Cuba Clearing Perilous Waters?*, 116.

[43] Gonzalez, *Cuba Clearing Perilous Waters?*, 116.

[44] Gonzalez, *Cuba Clearing Perilous Waters?* , 114.

[45] Gonzalez, *Cuba Clearing Perilous Waters?* , 114.

[46] Gonzalez, *Cuba Clearing Perilous Waters?*, 118.

[47] Gonzalez, *Cuba Clearing Perilous Waters?*, 117.

[48] Gonzalez, *Cuba Clearing Perilous Waters?* , 117.

[49] Gonzalez, *Cuba Clearing Perilous Waters?* 117.

[50] Gonzalez, *Cuba Clearing Perilous Waters?*, 111.

[51] Gonzalez, *Cuba Clearing Perilous Waters?* , 114.

[52] Gonzalez, *Cuba Clearing Perilous Waters?*, 117.

[53] Gonzalez, *Cuba Clearing Perilous Waters?*, 117.

[54] Gonzalez, *Cuba Clearing Perilous Waters?* , 117.

[55] Gonzalez, *Cuba Clearing Perilous Waters?* , 118.

[56] Gonzalez, *Cuba Clearing Perilous Waters?* , 117.

[57] Doreen Hemlock, "Behind Elian Smokescreen, Repression in Cuba, *Sun Sentinel*, 12 January, 2000 [article on-line accessed April 6, 2000] *CubaNet News*; available at http://www.cubanet.org/; Internet.

[58]Gonzalez, *Cuba Clearing Perilous Waters?*, 118.

[59] Ernesto Betancourt, "How Will the Castro Regime End?"; paper presented at a luncheon sponsored by the Institute for Cuban and Cuban American Studies at the University of Miami, Coral Gables, Florida.

[60] Betancourt, "How Will the Castro Regime End?"

[61] Betancourt, "How Will the Castro Regime End?"

[62] Betancourt, "How Will the Castro Regime End?"

[63] Betancourt, "How Will the Castro Regime End?"

[64] Betancourt, "How Will the Castro Regime End?"

[65] Gonzalez and Nucio, *The RAND Forum on Cu*ba, 41.

[66] Edward Gonzalez and Thomas S. Szayna, *"Cuba and Lessons Learned from Other Communist Transitions: A Workshop Repor*t" (Santa Monica: RAND Corporation, 1998), 27.

Notes

[67] Gonzalez and Szayna, *"Cuba and Lessons Learned from Other Communist Transitions: A Workshop Report"* (Santa Monica, RAND Corporation, 1998), 27.

[68] Gonzalez and Szayna, *"Cuba and Lessons Learned from Other Communist Transitions: A Workshop Report"*, 41.

PART VII

ASSESSMENT OF THE CURRENT POLICY

The US' Cuba policy, since 1898, has been reactionary in nature lacking coherence and consistency. The current policies need to be institutionalized via a process that will provide a continuous review and, more importantly, ensure coherency and consistency. US policy must be based on the US' national interest, support its national security and advocate the humanitarian principles upon which the nation was founded. Additionally, the policy needs to identify and correlate long-term, mid-term and short-term objectives to ensure the US is prepared to respond to Castro's customary (short-term) political provocations, to assist in Cuba in its transition to a post-Castro government (mid- and long term issues) and to protect the US national security and national interests upon the inevitable demise of the Castro regime (long-term).

The US and Cuba have an economic and political history dating back to the early nineteenth century. These interests have not changed much since the now defunct Monroe Doctrine of 1823 declared, "with the movements in this hemisphere we [of the Western hemisphere] are of necessity more immediately connected; and by causes which must be obvious to all enlightened and impartial observers."[1] The US' response to the Cuban Missile Crisis and the subsequent aberration of the principles embodied in the Monroe Doctrine after the demise of the Soviet Union have made any reference to the

Monroe Doctrine taboo. These two little words convey images of economic and political relations and covert actions that resulted in the economic and political subjugation of Latin American nations to the US and to the support of abusive, totalitarian regimes under the auspices of containing the communist threat.[2] Moreover, the move toward political isolation that began in the 1960s following the Vietnam War left many with "a lingering feeling of historic guilt."[3] Now that there appears to be no reason to provide for an ideological or military defense from Russia, the US' Cuba policy is less coherent and consistent that ever.

Currently, the policy of the Clinton administration is "to promote a peaceful transition to democracy on the island."[4] In order to support the transition, the administration "is proceeding on a multi-faced track: pressure on the regime for change through the comprehensive economic embargo and LIBERTAD sanctions (Track One); outreach to the Cuban people (Track Two); the promotion and protection of human rights (Track Three); multilateral efforts to press for democracy (Track Four); and migration accords to promote safe, orderly and legal migration (Track Five)."[5] The underlying assumption is that these measures will lead to the attainment of our national interest or "a peaceful transition to democracy on the island."[6]

As they apply to the previous discussion on short-, mid-, and long-term objectives, the Track One measures would have to be classified as long term initiatives due to the fact that the economic embargo and LIBERTAD sanctions will not provide a short-term resolution. The Track Two outreach measures and Track Three human rights measures are unilateral and multi-lateral in nature and can be pursued as mid-term and long-term objectives respectively with little hope for resolution under the Castro regime. The Track

Four efforts to effect democratic reform of Cuba's polity and economy are more in line with multi-lateral, long-term objectives. Efforts to transition to a democratic government would have to build upon and be tied to economic reforms that would create, strengthen and empower a civil society. The Track Five migration accords fall in the category of bilateral short-term measures that may be readily negotiated and resolved. The people-to-people cultural exchanges, resumption of telephone and mail service and other issues that do not represent a threat to the regime and are not vital to US security or national interests, also fall in the short-term category.

In that regard, it is appropriate to review the measures adopted under each of the tracks and attempt to assess their probability for success in the short-, mid-, and long-term. Track One consists of applying "pressure on the regimes for change through the comprehensive embargo and LIBERTAD actions."[7] The economic embargo was imposed in 1960 in response to "the Cuban government's failure to compensate thousands of US companies and individuals whose properties, large and small, were confiscated after the revolution."[8]

Beginning with the Kennedy administration, the economic embargo was expanded in an attempt to affect the political and economic isolation and demise of the Castro regime. If US policy makers had possessed a better understanding of Castro's psyche as well as a better understanding of the Cuban culture, they would have known the embargo would not deter Castro from his chosen path or lead the Cuban people to influence his political behavior. However, in fairness to the embargo, "without sanctions, the United States would be virtually powerless to influence events absent war [and] sanctions may not be perfect and they are not always the answer but they are often the only weapon."[9]

Since the mid 1970s, but especially after the demise of the Soviet Union in 1991, there has been mounting criticism of the economic embargo. The more extremist among those who oppose the embargo believe the US, "by its unyielding campaign of forcing and international blockade, continued to use starvation as a political weapon against the Cuban people."[10] They also blame the embargo for the decline in the health of the Cuban people, shortages of food and consumer goods, and the decline of social mores. Contrary to popular belief, Cuba's current socio-economic problems are less a function of the embargo and more a result of the "inefficiencies of a centrally planned economy… isolation from the spur of competition in international markets resulting from the protective umbrella provided by the Soviet barter, and…large expenditures on military forces."[11]

The anti-embargo forces received momentum from those who oppose the Cuban Democracy (1992) and LIBERTAD (1996) Acts that not only strengthen economic sanctions, but also pledge economic support for a "free and independent Cuba."[12] US allies are particularly opposed to the Title Four provisions of the LIBERTAD Act that limit foreign investment in Cuba by opposing individuals and businesses trafficking in confiscated US properties.[13] They, like many in the US business sector, believe that improved economic relations and prosperity will lead to political reforms in Cuba. However, "economic considerations have never dominated Castro's policies [and] on the contrary, political considerations usually dictate economic policies."[14] If Castro were interested in the economic development and prosperity of Cuba and improving the quality of life of the Cuban people, he would not have closed the peasant markets or established a medical tourist industry and a splinter dollar economy, which make Cubans second-class citizens in their own country. He would also not continue to direct the harassment of the members of the independent agrarian cooperatives who are currently keeping the Cubans from starving.[15]

Those who believe foreign investment and International Monetary Fund loans could alter Castro's political behavior and improve the lives of the Cuban people would do well to research the Canadian's experience with Castro's version of joint ventures and the events which occurred in Cuba following the Pope's visit in March of 1998. Last year, FirstKeye Project Technologies, a Canadian-based firm, entered into a $500 million agreement to improve Cuba's electric power system and lost $9million dollars when Castro reneged on the deal keeping the plans that he is used to lure other foreign contractors.[16] In regards to quality of life of the Cuban people, the Pope's visit did not deter Castro from the waves of political repression accompanying the trials of the members of the Internal Dissidents' Working Group (1998) and the Ibero-American Summit (November 1999).

Admittedly, the economic embargo has failed to bring about political or economic change in Cuba. However, the embargo should not be judged and abrogated on these terms. Rather, US policy makers should focus on the original impetus for economic sanctions and maintain the embargo for two reasons. First, forty years after Castro expropriated US property, the 5,911 claims certified by the US Claims Commission valued at $12 billion as of June 1998 (simple interest accrues at 6%)[17] have never been settled. Secondly, by considering abrogation of the economic embargo, US policy makers are signaling a lack of resolve. The embargo is a political symbol to US citizens, Cubans, Cuban-Americans and Latin Americans alike. Beyond that, just as "a market economy and political freedom are not the same thing",[18] the US "should [advocate] political freedom not capitalism."[19]

If the embargo were abrogated, it would be the equivalent of condoning nationalist expropriation and relinquishing debts owed to the US government and its citizens. Moreover, lofty arguments on the failure of the embargo to effect political and economic change and the negative impact it has on the Cuban people are not even accepted by the learned Cuban population. Cuban citizens know the embargo exacerbates the island's balance of trade and balance of payments problems and that the embargo limits the government's access to international money markets increasing the cost of imports.[20] However, they also know "the communist system is the origin and the cause of the Cuban's grave situation"[21] and suspect that US efforts to lift the embargo are not motivated by humanitarian concerns, but by US business interests that seek "to enrich US businesses at the expense of the sweat of Cuban workers."[22]

The economic embargo should be maintained and classified as a long-term objective in support of the US policy "to promote a peaceful transition to democracy."[23] In the long-term, it may be a useful tool in negotiations with a post-Castro government.

The second track of the administration's Cuba policy promotes "outreach to the Cuban people"[24] to "ease their plight and help them prepare for a democratic future."[25] The outreach measures include cultural and scientific exchanges as well as expansion of remittances and additional charter flights to Cuba as well as the sale of food to Cuban NGOs. These measures have improved the lives of the segment of the Cuban population that has relatives in the US who travel to Cuba with consumer goods and American dollars or who send money on a regular basis.[26] There is a lot of controversy surrounding this issue in that although the remittances and visits may help the Cuban people, they invariably put money in the government coffers. Also, the dollarization of the economy has fragmented Cuban society creating two distinct groups, those who have access to dollars via exile relatives or the tourist industry and those who do not. Additionally, in Cuba, the government must authorize NGOs and organizations that operate without authorization are prosecuted under the penal law. In effect, these NGOs are under state control and any US contributions made to these organizations will be filtered through government agencies.[27]

The Track Two measures should be reviewed with the intent to develop short-, mid- and long-term objectives that reach out to the fledgling civil society and those organizations that are unable to obtain NGO status from the government. Moreover, the issue of visits and remittances should be reviewed with an eye toward minimizing the benefit derived by the Cuban government.

The Third Track calls for "the protection of human rights"[28] which the US has advocated before the United Nations. In April of 1998, the Commission failed to condemn human rights violations in Cuba for the first time in seven years. Moreover, it eliminated the "special rapporteur" or oversight function. In March of 1999, the sentencing of the Leaders of the Internal Dissidents Working Group that published "The Homeland Belongs to Us All" drew criticism from the European Community. However, European direct investment and trade with Cuba continued to grow. [29] As of January of this year, there were an estimated 350 political prisons in Cuba. By 1998, Cuba was reported to be operating 41 maximum-security prisons, 30 minimum-security prisons, and 200 work camps; a combined total of 271 correctional facilities.[30] In comparison, the

State of Texas, which, as of August of 1999 had a population of 20.1 million, has 99 correction facilities. Conditions in the Cuban prisons are deplorable and the "prison population [lives] in substandard unhealthy conditions, where prisoners face physical and sexual abuse."[31] In April of this year, the United Nations reversed its 1998 position and condemned Cuba for its human rights violations. Cuban prisoners of conscience deserve the concerted attention of the international community and the US should continue to advocate for their legal rights, humane treatment, and release. Track Three policies should be pursued as short- and mid-term objectives. Although this issue is not likely to result in a short-term resolution, it deserves immediate effort.

The Fourth Track commits to pursue "multilateral efforts to press for democracy." [32] In 1996, the US obtained the EU's support in adopting a "Common Position on Cuba"[33] that pledges economic assistance of a democratic transition; however, the EC's support of the administration's democracy policy will invariably be affected if a future administration should decide to implement the provisions of Title Four of the LIBERTAD Act. The EU has officially opposed Cuba's political oppression and human rights violations; however, its continued investment and trade with Cuba despite Cuba's dismal record on "forming independent unions or bargaining collectively [make] the European companies as well as all foreign investors in Cuba complicit in the Cuban government's human rights violations."[34] The Track Four measures related to conditions of labor can be reviewed as mid-term objectives in conjunction with US allies. However, the joint venture structure imposed by the Cuban government will most likely impair a mid- to long-term resolution. The recognition of organizations that have

139

been unable to obtain NGO status can also be reviewed as a Track Four mid-term objective.

Finally, the Fifth Track resulted in a migration agreement in 1994 between the US and Cuba that provides for "safe, orderly and legal migration"[35] whereby the US agreed to accept a minimum of 20,000 immigrants per year and, in turn, Cuba agreed to take steps to curtail unauthorized departures.[36] The 20,000 minimum is reached by sequential processing of the following categories:

1. Non-immigrant Visas: for temporary visits
2. Immigrant Visas: for family members of US citizens or US residents (Visa applicants are required to obtain government approval to leave Cuba)
3. Refugee Program: for those who can demonstrate they are persecuted based on their race, religion or political ideology (Limit of 3,000 per year)
4. Lottery: for those who do not otherwise qualify to complete the 20,000 minimum
5. Humanitarian and Special Paroles: for those who do not otherwise qualify at the discretion of the US Attorney General[37]

In effect, this agreement modified the Cuban Adjustment Act of 1966 that permitted any Cuban who was "inspected, admitted or paroled into the United States"[38] subsequent to January 1, 1959 to apply for permanent residency after one year. "Inspected and admitted"[39] applies to those who entered the US legally via a non-immigrant visa or under some other legal status and "paroled" refers to the US Attorney General's discretion in, for example, humanitarian cases whereby the Attorney General "can allow and alien without legal status to come into and remain in the United States temporarily."[40]

However, general migration policy was restricted under the Reagan and Bush administrations[41] and by executive orders, interdiction policies were established that suspended the admission of "aliens from the high seas"[42] and permitted "the forced return of interdicted aliens."[43]   In accordance with Section 212(f) of the Immigration and Nationality Act of 1952 as amended:

> Whenever the President finds that entry of any aliens or of any class of aliens into the United States would be detrimental to the interests of the United States, he may by proclamation…suspend the entry of all aliens or any class of aliens as immigrants or non-immigrants, or impose on the entry of aliens any restrictions he may deem appropriate.[44]

Thus, the basis for the repatriation of Cubans is that "no alien is entitled to parole"[45] and the Act [Cuban Adjustment Act of 1966] provides a procedure for seeking permanent residency, not an entitlement to it."[46] However, the interdiction policy does not preclude "an alien from [applying] for asylum once physically on our shores."[47]

In May of 1995, the Clinton administration agreed to accept the 30,000 Cubans who had been held at Guantanamo since 1994 and to "intercept future Cuban migrants attempting to enter the United States by sea and would return them to Cuba."[48] In accordance with this agreement, "refugees who are intercepted before they reach [dry land in] the United States are returned to Cuba."[49] Although there is undoubtedly a need to restrain uncontrolled migration into the US, this policy created a dangerous situation for those attempting to flee Cuba and the US Coast Guard charged with the implementation of this policy. The June 1999 incident in which the Coast Guard used pepper spray and a water canon to prevent Cubans from touching land in Florida[50] is an example to the implications of a reactionary policy.

In effect, the Refugee Act of 1980 requires Cubans who are not eligible to apply for an immigrant visa, to prove he or she is the subject of persecution without regard to the island's political system.[51] Therefore, there should not be any exception to the process of applying for refugee admission. The current policy of exempting those who reach "dry land" while interdicting those whose feet are in water is dangerous. Additionally, as we have seen in the case of Haitians and Elian Gonzalez, the Attorney General's Special Parole Authority by which "illegal" aliens are granted parole or asylum is highly discretionary and should be reviewed as a short- or mid-term objective with the intent to develop a coherent and consistent policy for all those seeking asylum in the US.

In sum, the policies of the Clinton administration have yet to achieve the US national interest "to promote a peaceful transition to democracy on the island."[52] The administration has, to date, focused on Track Two "outreach" and Track Five migration issues. These people-to-people measures are well intended; however, they will fall short of establishing and empowering a civil society capable of forming a viable opposition. These measures will alleviate the suffering of some and highlight the continuing need of others. For as long as Castro maintains repressive control over the society, it will be impossible to promote "a peaceful democratic transition in Cuba from the successful initiatives of Cubans on the island to build civil society and promote respect for human rights."[53]

Castro remains a radical nationalist and revolutionary with blinding anti-American predilections. He has, time and again, asserted his commitment to the paths of revolution and socialism or, in effect, Castroism. In light of his unwavering commitment, US policy makers should be cognizant of the dangers shadowed by a false sense of security and resist the complacency resulting from political fatigue.

US policy makers must develop a cohesive and consistent Cuba policy for dealing with the current regime and consider that eventually nature will take its course; Castro will die. Therefore, it is in the US national interest to develop a process for the continuous review of Cuban affairs to ensure that Cuba policy is prepared for the turmoil that is certain to accompany the demise of the Castro regime.

Notes

[1] The Monroe Doctrine.

[2] Gaddis Smith, *The Last Years of the Monroe Doctrine, 1945-1993* (New York: Hill and Wang, 1994), 4-7.

[3] Horowitz, *"Paradox, Procrastination, and Paralysis,"*, 3.

[4] Michael Ranneberger; Statement to the Department of State to the House Ways and Means Committee Subcommittee on Trade, May 7, 1998 [on-line accessed April 26, 2000], available at http://usembassy.state.gov/posts/cu1/wwwh0037.html; Internet.

[5] Horowitz, *"Paradox, Procrastination, and Paralysis,"* 3.

[6] Horowitz, *"Paradox, Procrastination, and Paralysis,"* 3.

[7] Ranneberger Statement.

[8] Ranneberger Statement.

[9] Jesse Helms, "What Sanctions Epidemic", *Foreign Affairs*, January/February 1999.

[10] Simons, 39.

[11] Charles Wolf Jr., *"International Economic Sanctions"* (Santa Monica: RAND Corporation, 1980), 3.

[12] Cuban Liberty and Democratic Solidarity Act (LIBERTAD) 22 U.S. Code 22, Chapter 69A, Subchapter 2, Assistance to a Free and Independent Cuba (1992) [code on-line accessed April 20, 2000], available at http://law2house.gov/uscode-cgi/fastweb.exe?Search; Internet.

[13] Sullivan, "Cuba: Issues for Congress", CRS-8.

[14] Jaime Suchlicki, *Cuba: A Current Assessment*, 9.

[15] Manuel David Orrio, "Los Guajiros Tambien Gritan Libertad!" *CubaNet* News [on line accessed 4 May 4, 2000], available at http://www.cubanet.org/cooperativa/articulo.html; Internet.

[16] Jose de Cordoba and Carlta Vitzhu, "No Cigar For Jilted Engineers from Canada, Cuba Wasn't a Cheap Date", *Wall Street Journal*, June 28, 1999.

[17] G. Douglas Harper, "Restitution of Property in Cuba: Lessons Learned from East Europe," in *Association for the Study of the Cuban Economy (ASCE): Papers and Proceedings of the Ninth Annual Meeting for the Study of the Cuban Economy (ASCE),* in Coral Gables, Florida, august 12-14 1999, vol. 9 (Silver Spring: Association for the Study of the Cuban Economy (ASCE) 1999), 1-11.

[18] Charley Reese, "A Free Market Economy Doesn't Always Mean a Free Country." *The Orlando Sentinel*, July 22, 1999.

[19] Reese, "A Free Market Economy Doesn't Always Mean a Free Country."

[20] Concilio Cubano, *"Plataforma Comun,"* [on-line accessed February 13, 2000], available at http//www.exilio.com/DOC3/dignidad_N.html); Internet.

[21] Cooperative of Cuban Independent Correspondents. "Al Pueblo Americano," [declaration on-line accessed February 13, 2000], available at http: //www.exilio.com/DOC3/dignidad_N.html); Internet.

[22] "Al Pueblo Americano"

[23] Ranneberger Statement.

[24] Ranneberger Statement.

[25] "People-to-People" Fact Sheet.

[26] "People-to-People" Fact Sheet.

Notes

[27] Human Rights Watch Report.

[28] Ranneberger Statement.

[29] Human Rights Watch Report.

[30] Human Rights Watch Report.

[31] Human Rights Watch Report.

[32] Ranneberger Statement.

[33] "US-Cuba History".

[34] Human Rights Watch Report.

[35] U.S. Agency for International Development (USAID) "*USAID/Cuba Program: January 2000,*" [on-line accessed on February 12, 2000] available at http://www.info. usaid.gov/countries/cu/upd-cub.htm; Internet.

[36] "Migration Fact Sheet."

[37] "Migration Fact Sheet."

[38] Larry M. Eig, "Cuban Migration: Legal Basics," CRS Report for Congress, (Congressional Research Service, The Library of Congress, 1999), CRS-3.

[39] Eig, CRS-3.

[40] Eig, CRS-3.

[41] Eig, CRS-4.

[42] Eig, CRS-4.

[43] Eig, CRS-5.

[44] Eig, CRS-4.

[45] Eig, CRS-4.

[46] Eig, CRS-3.

[47] Eig, CRS-5.

[48] Sullivan, CRS-8.

[49] "Fix Rafter Policy to Reduce Risk", Editorial, *Sun Sentinel*, October 11, 1999.

[50] Sullivan, CRS-13-14.

[51] U.S. Interests Section, Havana, Cuba, [document on-line] accessed on February 12, 2000; Internet available at http://usembassy.state.gov/posts/cu1/wwwhooo2.html.

[52] Ranneberger Statement.

[53] Ranneberger Statement.

PART VIII

PROPOSAL FOR POLICY REVIEW PROCESS

When Castro is finally consecrated to the pages of history, will the Cuban people be prepared to establish the constitutional democracy they have been longing for since 1868? What, if any, will be the role of the US? "Whatever its composition, any successor regime is certain to be weaker and less cohesive that when Fidel Castro was present."[1] However, "if it is to survive, a post-Castro regime would need to embark on a new course that holds out the prospect of a rapid economic recovery for the Cuban people."[2]

One estimate calls for about $10 billion for "economic reconstruction"[3] and an additional $5 billion "in the form of emergency loans"[4] to make immediate improvements in the quality of life of the Cuban people and fuel an economic recovery program. The economy program would initially be a short-term objective; however, as the emergency measures are achieved, the planning should precede as a mid- and long-term process to ensure that economic measures are supported by appropriate social, political, and economic measures.

However, US assistance should not be limited to economic aid. The US has an abundance of human resources that can assist Cuba in the process of "reconstruction and development"[5] "decollectivization,"[6] and "desocialization"[7] process. According to Jorge, "a first point of extraordinary importance is the adequate coordination of the means of structural change (organizations and institutions) with those of policy and stabilization (monetary and fiscal policies and also those related to subsidies and foreign exchange among others)."[8] Jorge emphasizes the importance of Cuba's cultural history and, in this context, the social and political systems that will govern the economy. Moreover, he stipulates the success of economic reforms will depend on the nature of the transition plan and should follow a "gradualist organic process."[9] That is, the transition plan should identify required economic changes and linkages to Cuba's social, political and legal systems. The plan should also prioritize the required changes and identify their order and timing.

Jorge estimates the economic restructuring phase will take about five years[10] and that "the achiles heel in this area [economic reconstruction and development] would be represented by (a) inappropriate economic motivations and attitudes...and (b) the unavailability of sufficient entrepreneurial talent."[11] In light of Cuba's political, social and economic isolation over the last forty years, it would be prudent to acknowledge its limitations and to compliment its capabilities. Cuba lacks material resources; however, "there is no doubt that sufficient human talent exists in Cuba."[12] Moreover, "given the appropriate economic motivations and attitudes [resulting from] an immediate increase in the levels of consumption"[13] and with the assistance of the US and its allies, the Cuban people would be able to implement the required economic social and political reforms.

In order to assist the Cuban people and to successfully pursue the current Cuba policy goal, the US government should establish a matrix organization or commission funded through the U.S. Agency for International Development (USAID) for the purpose of reviewing policy objectives and identifying their relevance, priority and timing vis-à-vis the US policy goal. USAID currently promotes " a peaceful transition to democracy in Cuba"[14] via funding to US organizations that support Cuban human rights activists, independent journalists, independent Cuban NGOs, and many others.[15]

Assuming the US will continue, "to promote a peaceful transition to democracy in Cuba"[16] then, the Clinton administration's five-track policies should be viewed as objectives that in the short-, mid- or long-term, would contribute to the attainment of the overriding policy goal. Although the use of the words "goal" and "objectives" may be interpreted as semantics, the proposed terminology makes it clear that measures such as the embargo are "objectives" to pursue in the eventual attainment of the overriding "policy goal." Moreover, it makes it easier to understand that no single objective, such as the embargo, will lead to the attainment of the policy goal. Furthermore, the identification, prioritization, and sequencing of short, mid, and long-term objectives would help to explain apparent dichotomies between short- and mid- and long-term objectives in pursuit of the overriding policy goal.

One of the major criticisms of the Clinton administration's Track Two "outreach" measures is that, by helping the Cuban people through the increase of remittances, the US is also helping the economy of Cuba keeping the Castro regime afloat. While this may be the case in the short-term, the "outreach" measures, if viewed as long-term objectives, are intended to help the Cuban people in their transition to democracy. In other words, they are intended to enable the Cuban people to "live to fight another day."

It is essential that the proposed organization tasked to conduct the policy review be a matrix or organization that combines experts from the following organizations that represent the following government offices:

1. Senate and House of Representatives
2. USAID Cuba Desk
3. Department of State, Cuba Desk
4. Office of Inter American Affairs
5. Department of Defense
6. National Security Council, Cuba Office
7. Central Intelligence Agency, Cuba Office
8. Treasury Department

The organization should also include experts in, at a minimum, the following fields:

1. Health
2. Law (Civil, Military, Electoral, Labor, etc.)
3. Education
4. Economy (Agriculture, Industry, Commerce, Trade, etc.)
5. Transportation
6. Communications (Public Relations, Computers, Telephone, etc.)
7. Finance (Banking, Stock Market, etc.)
8. Tourism
9. Religion
10. Social Sciences (Race, Ethnicity, Values, Corruption)

The members of this organization, at all levels, should be experts in their fields or selected to participate based on their background and experience. In addition, every effort should be made to ensure that they represent varying perspectives on the issues. The proposed matrix organization, from this point on referred to as the Cuban Matrix, would consist of an Executive Committee led by a chairperson from the USAID (See Figure 1) and a co-chairperson assigned tasked to coordinate the activities of the sub-committees on behalf of the sponsoring government agency, USAID, and the chairperson.

The University of Miami's Institute for Cuban and Cuban-American Studies (ICCAS) is in an ideal position to serve as the coordinating activity due to its physical proximity to Cuba, its access to sources of information, its extensive political, academic and business networks, and its ongoing activity in the area of Cuban transition studies.

The functions of the Cuba Matrix would be carried out by two committees: the Committee for Contingency Plans and the Committee for Transition Plans (See Figure 1). The Committee for Contingency Plans would be responsible for reviewing developments in Cuban affairs and developing scenarios and proposed solutions for those scenarios that, in the short-term, would impact US national security or national interests. If required, it would draw members from the Committee for Transition Plans in order to develop contingency plans. Initially, this committee would focus on issues that or of short-term impact to US security of national interests. Later, it would incorporate the findings of the Transition Committee in developing mid to long-term contingency plans.

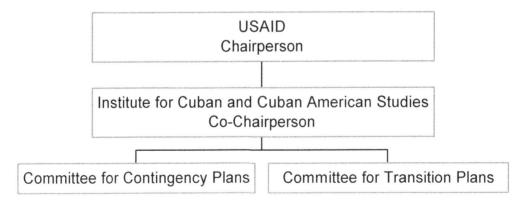

Figure 1: The Cuban Matrix

The sub-committees should be formed along functional lines (See Figure 2). That is, there should be a sub-committee chartered to study economic reforms that could, in turn, be further divided to study agricultural and industrial reforms, privatization of business and housing etc. Other committees would be tasked to review social (education, health) and political (electoral, human rights) reforms. As part of the Cuban Matrix, the committees would be responsible for feeding the results of their reviews to each other as well as the Executive Board.

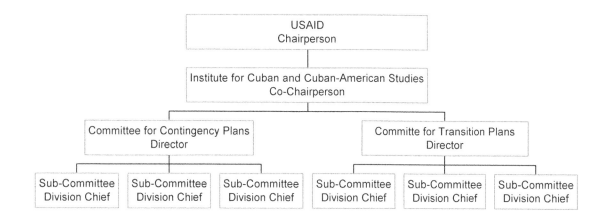

Figure 2: Cuban Matrix Subcommittees

As part of an ongoing process, the subcommittees would identify required reforms within their own functional areas, prioritize them, and identify linkages or areas that impact or require input from other sub-committees. The findings would be provided to the Co-Chairperson or coordinating activity to chair a meeting of the committees involved and to ensure a coordinated plan is prepared for presentation to the Executive Board.

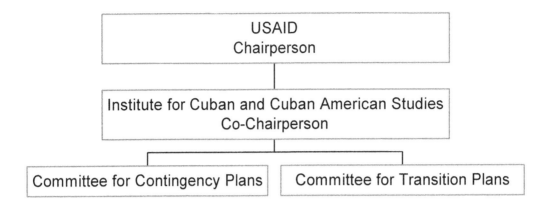

Figure 3: Cuban Matrix Executive Committee

Each committee would have to proceed from a clear understanding of the overriding

US policy goal and review, identify, and classify each objective in accordance with its

sequence (short, mid, or long-term) in attaining the policy goal.

This proposal would require high-level approval and a significant fiscal commitment.

Initially, the Cuban Matrix, at the Executive Board level, should focus on a review of the

policy goal and if still valid, a review of the current policy objectives (5-track policies) to

ensure they represent a coherent and consistent approach that, based on their sequence,

(short, mid or long-term), contribute to the attainment of the policy goal.

The proposed Cuban Matrix may appear to be a cumbersome hierarchical structure;

however, its main purpose is to ensure there is competent, diverse, overlapping and

coordinated participation. Undoubtedly, there may be fiscal, logistics and existing

organizational constraints. Their identification and potential resolution is well outside the

scope of this paper. The purpose of presenting the proposal is two-fold: 1) to highlight the fact that the US Cuba policy is unnecessarily reactive and lacks a process by which it can be made more coherent and consistent and 2) to propose a model for the institutionalization of a participative process that might not only produce a coherent and consistent policy, but also provide for its continuous review.

Notes

[1] Gonzalez and Nuccio, *"The RAND Forum on Cuba"*, 51.

[2] Gonzalez and Nuccio, *"The RAND Forum on Cuba"*, 51

[3] Antonio Jorge, *A Reconstruction Strategy for Post-Castro Cuba* (North –South Center for Research Studies, University of Miami, 1993), 8.

[4] Jorge, *A Reconstruction Strategy for Post-Castro Cuba,* 8.

[5] Jorge, *A Reconstruction Strategy for Post-Castro Cuba,* 8.

[6] Jorge, *A Reconstruction Strategy for Post-Castro Cuba,* 11.

[7] Jorge, *A Reconstruction Strategy for Post-Castro Cuba,* 11.

[8] Jorge, *A Reconstruction Strategy for Post-Castro Cuba,* 5.

[9] Jorge, *A Reconstruction Strategy for Post-Castro Cuba,* 13.

[10] Jorge, *A Reconstruction Strategy for Post-Castro Cuba,* 5.

[11] Jorge, *A Reconstruction Strategy for Post-Castro Cuba,* 10.

[12] Jorge, *A Reconstruction Strategy for Post-Castro Cuba,* 13.

[13] Jorge, *A Reconstruction Strategy for Post-Castro Cuba,* 10.

[14] "USAID/Cuba Program."

[15] "USAID/Cuba Program."

[16] Ranneberger Statement.

PART IX

CONCLUSION

Past, present and future...; the fate of the Cuban people will continue to rest with those who live on that small island ninety miles off the Florida coast. In a historical perspective, their Spanish culture and nurture as well as their subsequent dependence on the United States contributed to their lack of responsibility and acquiescence to a state of helplessness. Today, Cubans are pre-occupied with their daily subsistence and survival. They are totally controlled by Castro's security forces and their dissidence is likely to remain passive in nature.

Castro's "Cubanization" efforts in Latin America and other Third World countries made Cuba a "fly in the ointment" of the United States; however, with the exception of the Cuban Missile Crisis, Cuba has not been a serious threat to the US national security. Recently, his revolutionary activities have been forcibly constrained. Nevertheless, he remains a threat to US national interests by virtue of his physical proximity, his potential command of vital sea lanes, and his impact on migration and drug trafficking activities. He also poses a potential threat to the US national security as evidenced by Cuba's biological warfare and electronic interception capabilities.

Current US policy focuses on people-to-people measures designed to help the Cuban people transition to democracy. However, these long-term measures have yet to create or empower a civil society empowered to pursue this goal. Nature will take its course and Castro will die. Those who are ninety miles away and more may wish to believe that nothing short of an attack or a violent overthrow will affect them; however, they would be diluting themselves.

The question is not should the US be involved? The question is, when and how will the US be involved? Any organization and process designed to review US policy and to develop coherent and consistent objectives would constitute a proactive step to guide the US' inevitable involvement in Cuba's future development. In the end, Mario Lazo's words are the most relevant:

> It is indisputable that the United States cannot avoid involvement in the affairs of other nations. The great power which it wields by virtue of its prestige, wealth, and strength makes intervention necessary. When it gives economic aid it intervenes. When it withholds such aid, as in the case of the Cuban arms embargo, it also intervenes...the question therefore, is not whether is should or should not intervene *but whether a particular intervention is desirable.*[2]

---

[2] Lazo, 186.

BIBLIOGRAPHY

Alvarez, Jose. "Independent Agricultural Cooperatives in Cuba?" In *Association for the Study of the Cuban Economy (ASCE): Papers and Proceedings of the Ninth Annual Meeting of the Association for the Study of the Cuban Economy (ASCE) in Coral Gables, Florida, August 12-14, 1999,* vol. 9, 157-164. Silver Spring: Association for the Study of the Cuban Economy.

Betancourt, Ernesto. "How Will the Regime End." Paper presented at a luncheon sponsored by the Institute for Cuban and Cuban-American Studies at the University of Miami, Coral Gables, Florida

Betancourt, Ernesto and Guillermo Grenier. "Measuring Cuban Public Opinion: Economic, Social and Political Issues." In *Association for the Study of the Cuban Economy (ASCE): Papers and Proceedings of the Ninth Annual Meeting of the Association for the Study of the Cuban Economy (ASCE) in Coral Gables, Florida, August 12-14, 1999,* vol. 9, 251-269. Silver Spring: Association for the Study of the Cuban Economy.

Bonsal, Philip W. *Cuba, Castro and the United States.* University of Pittsburg Press, 1972.

Cardoba, Jose and Carlta Vitzhum. "No Cigar: For Jilted Engineers from Canada, Cuba Wasn't a Cheap Date." *The Wall Street Journal,* June 28, 1999.

Castro, Fidel. "History Will Absolve Me." Extract printed in Geoff Simons, *Cuba from Conquistador to Castro,* app. 6, p. 356. New York: St Martin's Press, 1996.

Castro, Fidel. "First Havana Declaration." Extract printed in Geoff Simons, *Cuba from Conquistador to Castro,* app. 6, p. 356. New York: St Martin's Press, 1996.

Concilio Cubano. "Plataforma Comun." Document on-line. Available at http://www.exilio.com/DOC3/dignidad_N.html; Internet.

Cooperative of Cuban Independent Correspondents. *"Al Pueblo Americano."* Declaration on-line. Available at http://www.exilio.com/DOC3/dignidad_N.html; Internet.

Cuban Liberty and Democratic Solidarity Act (LIBERTAD). 22 U.S. Code 22, Chapter 69A, SubChapter 2, Assistance to a Free and Democratic Cuba (1996). Code on-line. Available at http://law2house.gov/uscode-cgi/fastweb.exe?search; Internet.

Eig, Larry M. "Cuban Migration: Legal Basics: CRS Report for Congress." Congressional Research Service, The Library of Congress, 1999.

Falcoff, Marc. "Cuban Medicine and Foreign Patients." *Cuba Brief,* Summer 1998.

Fontaine, Roger W. *On Negotiating with Cuba.* Washington D.C: American Institute for Public Policy Research, 1975.

Gonzalez, Edward. *A Strategy for Dealing with Cuba in the 1980s.* Santa Monica: The RAND Corporation, 1992.

Gonzalez, Edward and David Ronfeldt. *Castro, Cuba, and the World.* Santa Monica: The RAND Corporation, 1986.

_____. *Cuba Adrift in a Post-Communist World.* Santa Monica: The RAND Corporation, 1992.

_____. *Cuba Clearing Perilous Waters?* Santa Monica: The RAND Corporation, 1996.

_____. *Storm Warnings for Cuba.* Santa Monica: The RAND Corporation, 1994.

Gonzalez, Edward and Thomas S. Szayna. *Cuba and Lessons Learned from Other Communist Transitions.* Santa Monica: The RAND Corporation, 1998.

Gonzalez, Emilio T. *"The Cuban Connection: Drug Trafficking and the Castro Regime."* In Cuban Studies vol. 2, no. 6 (July 15, 1997).

Harper, G. Douglas. "Restitution of Property in Cuba: Lessons Learned from East Europe." In *Association for the Study of the Cuban Economy (ASCE): Papers and Proceedings of the Ninth Annual Meeting of the Association for the Study of the Cuban Economy (ASCE) in Coral Gables, Florida, August 12-14, 1999,* vol. 9, 409-424. Silver Spring: Association for the Study of the Cuban Economy.

Helms, Jesse. "What Sanctions Epidemic?" *Foreign Affairs,* January/February 1999.

Horowitz, Irving Louis. American Foreign Policy Toward Castro's Cuba: Paradox, Procrastination, and Paralysis," in *The Conscience of Worms and the Cowardice of Lions.* New Brunswick: Transaction Publishers, 1992.

_____. "The Conscince of Castrologists: Thirty-Three Years of Solitude." in *The Conscience of Worms and the Cowardice of Lions.* New Brunswick: Transaction Publishers, 1992.

Human Rights Watch. *Cuba's Repressive Machinery: Human Rights for Forty Years After the Revolution.* Document on-line. Available at http://www.hrw.org/hrw/Reports/1999/cuba.htm; Internet.

Jacobs, Francine. *The Tainos: The People Who Welcomed Columbus.* New York: G.P. Putnam's Sons, 1992.

Jorge, Antonio. *A Reconstruction Strategy for Post-Castro Cuba: A Preliminary Outline of the Strategies for Reconstruction and Development in the Process of Decollectivization and Desocialization.* University of Miami North-South Center, 1991.

_____. *"The U.S. Embargo and the Failure of the Cuban Economy."* In the Institute for Cuban and Cuban-American Studies (ICCAS) Occasional Paper Series (February 2000).

Kennedy, John F. Quoted in Mario Lazo, *American Foreign Policy Failures in Cuba Dagger in the Heart,* 241. Pittsburg: University of Pittsburg Press; 1971

Lazo, Mario. *American Policy Failures In Cuba Dagger in the Heart.* New York City: Twin Circle Publishing Company, 1968.

Manifesto and Programme of 26 July Movement. Extract provided in Geoffrey Simons, *The Conscience of Worms and the Cowardice of Lions.* New Brunswick: Transaction Publishers, 1992.

Matthews, Herbert L. Quoted in Mario Lazo, *American Policy Failures in Cuba Dagger in the Heart,* 125. New York: Twin Circle Publishing, 1968.

Maybarduk, Gary H. "The State of the Cuban Economy 1998-1999." In *Association for the Study of the Cuban Economy (ASCE): Papers and Proceedings of the Ninth Annual Meeting of the Association for the Study of the Cuban Economy (ASCE) in Coral Gables, Florida, August 12-14, 1999,* vol. 9, 282-288. Silver Spring: Association for the Study of the Cuban Economy.

Messina, William A. Jr. "Agricultural Reform in Cuba: Implications for Agricultural Production, Markets and Trade." In *Association for the Study of the Cuban Economy (ASCE): Papers and Proceedings of the Ninth Annual Meeting of the Association for the Study of the Cuban Economy (ASCE) in Coral Gables, Florida, August 12-14, 1999,* vol. 9, 433-441. Silver Spring: Association for the Study of the Cuban Economy.

"Modificaciones al Codigo Penal de las Republica de Cuba." Available from *CubaNet* at http://www.cubanet.org/; Internet.

Monroe Doctrine, December 2, 1823. The Avalon Project at Yale Law School, 1999. Document on-line. Available at http://www.yale.edu//lawweb/avalon/diplomacy/monroe.htm; Internet.

Molina, Hilda. "A Cuban Doctor Reports: Cuban Medicine Today." *Cuba Brief,* Summer, 1998.

Morley, Morris Hyman, *"Toward A Theory of Imperial Politics: United States Policy and the Processes of State Formation, Disintegration, and Consolidation in Cuba, 1898-1978."* Ph. D. diss., State University of New York at Binghamton, 1980.

Mutchler, David A. "USAID Program Mandate for Cuba." Document on-line. Available at http://www.info.usaid.gov/countries/cu/mand.cub.htm; Internet.

Olsen, Fred. *On the Trail of the Arawaks.* University of Oklahoma Press, 1974.

Orrio, Manuel David. "Los Guajiros Tambien Gritan Libertad!" *CubaNet News.* Available at http://www.cubanet.org/cooperativa/articulo.html; Internet

Oostindie, Gert. *"A Loss of Purpose: Crisis in Transition in Cuba."* In Cuban Studies Occasional Paper Series vol. 2, no. 2 (March 15, 1997).

Perez, Antonio Alonso. "Ponencia al Encuentro de Cooperativas Independientes: Medio Ambiente, Ecologia y Su Impacto al Campesino Cubano." *CubaNet News.* Available at http://www.cubanet.org/cooperativa/articulo.html/;Internet.

Perez, Hernandez Reynaldo. "Ponencia al Encuentro de Cooperativas Independientes: Politica de Precios y Compra de los Productos Agricolas por Parte del Estado as Sector Campesino." *CubaNet News.* Available at http://www.cubanet.org/cooperativa/articulo.html/;Internet.

The Platt Amendment. Quoted in Geoffrey Simons, *The Conscience of Worms and the Cowardice of Lions.* New Brunswick: Transaction Publishers, 1992.

Press, Larry. *Cuban Telecommunications, Computer Networking, and U.S. Policy Implications.* Santa Monica: The RAND Corporation, 1996.

Ranneberger, Michael. *Statement to the House Ways and Means Committee on Trade.* Statement on-line. Available at http://usembassy.state.gov/cu1/wwwhoo37.html; Internet.

Reese, Charley. "A Free Market Economy Doesn't Always Mean a Free Country." *The Orlando Sentinel, July 22, 1999.*

Roberts, Churchill. "Measuring Cuban Public Opinion: Methodology." In *Association for the Study of the Cuban Economy (ASCE): Papers and Proceedings of the Ninth Annual Meeting of the Association for the Study of the Cuban Economy (ASCE) in Coral Gables, Florida, August 12-14, 1999,* vol. 9, 245-248. Silver Spring: Association for the Study of the Cuban Economy.

Simons, Geoff. *Cuba from Conquistador to Castro.* New York: St Martin's Press, 1996.

Skoug, Kenneth N. *The United States and Cuba under Reagan and Shultz.* Westpoint: Praeger Publishers, 1996.

Smith, Gaddis. *The Last Years of the Monroe Doctrine 1945-1993.* New York: Hill and Wang, 1994.

Suarez, Andres. *Cuba: Castroism and Communism, 1959-1966.* Cambridge: The Massachusetts Institute of Technology Press, 1967.

Suchlicki, Jaime. *"Cuba: A Current Assessment."* In Cuban Studies Occasional Paper Series vol. 2, no.4 (May 15, 1997).

_____. *Cuba from Columbus to Castro and Beyond,*4th ed. Washington: Brassey's Inc., 1997.

Sullivan, Mark P. *"Cuba Issues for Congress, October 29, 1999."* Congressional Research Service (CRS): The Library of Congress, 1999.

The Treaty of Paris Between the United States and Spain. Document on-line. Available at http://www.yale.edu/lawweb/avalon/sp1898.htm; Internet

U.S. Agency for International Development (USAID). *"USAID/Cuba Program: January 2000." Document on-line. Available at http://www.info.usaid.gov/countries/cu* Upd-cub.htm; Internet.

"U.S. Cuba History." Document on-line. Available from http://uscubacommission. org/history/html; Internet.

U.S. Interest Section, "Migration Fact Sheet." Document on-line. Available at http://www/regions/wha/cuba/migration.htm; Internet.

U.S. Interest Section, "People-to-People Fact Sheet." Document on-line. Available at http://www.state.gov/regions/wha/cuba/people.htm; Internet.

Walker, Phyllis Greene, Edward Gonzalez and Richard Nuccio. "U.S. Interests and Stakes in Cuban Transition Outcomes." In *The RAND Forum on Cuba*. Forum held in Washington D.C. April 16-17, 1998, edited by Edward Gonzalez and Richard Nuccio, 12-18. Santa Monica: The RAND Corporation, 1999.

Wolf, Charles Jr. *International Economic Sanctions.* Santa Monica, The RAND Corporation, 1980.

CPSIA information can be obtained at www.ICGtesting.com
Printed in the USA
LVOW03s1809310315

432756LV00019B/305/P